William Carew Hazlitt, Henry Huth

Narrative of the Journey of an Irish Gentleman Through England

1752

William Carew Hazlitt, Henry Huth

Narrative of the Journey of an Irish Gentleman Through England
1752

ISBN/EAN: 9783744725514

Printed in Europe, USA, Canada, Australia, Japan

Cover: Foto ©Thomas Meinert / pixelio.de

More available books at **www.hansebooks.com**

NARRATIVE OF THE

JOURNEY OF AN IRISH GENTLEMAN

THROUGH ENGLAND IN

THE YEAR 1752.

EDITED FROM A CONTEMPORARY MANUSCRIPT,

WITH A FEW ILLUSTRATIVE NOTES.

LONDON:

PRINTED AT THE CHISWICK PRESS.

1869.

PREFACE.

IN the following pages are given the contents of a MS. volume which came into my poſſeſſion a ſhort time ago. It is an anonymous narrative of the journey of an Iriſh gentleman through England in the year 1752. From its familiar and unpretentious ſtyle, and from a certain diſregard of the moſt ordinary rules of ſyntax, it ſeems unlikely that it was written with a view to publication; indeed, at p. 54 the author diſclaims any ſuch intention; nor after the moſt diligent inquiry can I find that it has ever before appeared in print.

On looking through it, I thought that I had ſeldom read anything ſo curious for notices of travelling in England at that period, or ſo full of curious popular matter and deſcriptions of localities, efpecially interefting at this diftance of time, and it appeared to me that, flender as its pretenfions to literary merit might be, it was not unworthy of being preferved in type, if only to the extent of a few copies for private circulation.

It is eafy to perceive that the writer was a gentleman who entertained a not unfavourable opinion of his own capacity, merits, and appearance; but perhaps this very egotifm may be thought to give a value to his book which it would otherwife have wanted. The charaĉteriftic little touches which peep out at almoft every turn, and the ftrong perfonal colouring imparted to the defcriptions, conftitute indeed the principal charm and intereft in works of the prefent kind. The little volume has quite a Bofwellian vein of coxcombry running through it from beginning to end.

It has been found neceffary to amend the punctuation throughout, and even to remedy, to a certain extent, the confufion of moods, tenfes, and cafes into which the writer or copyift has fallen; but at the fame time no undue liberties have been taken with the text, which (with the exceptions indicated) has been printed exactly as it ſtands in the original, inſomuch that in ſeveral places forms of expreſſion which are obſolete, and even ungrammatical, have been left intact.

My thanks are due to my friend Mr. W. Carew Hazlitt, of Kenſington, for his aſſiſtance in preparing the volume for the preſs, as well as for ſome intereſting notes which he has added to it.

HENRY HUTH.

30, Prince's Gate,
   January, 1869.

DEDICATION.

MADAM,

ONE line from your fair hand is more perſuaſive with me than twenty volumes from another; and if I have neglected fulfilling my promiſe ſo long, be aſſured it was not out of a principle of ſeeming refractory to your entreaties, but the ſcruple I made of ſubmitting to your cenſure the few irregular notes of two or three months: however, I rather chooſe to betray my ill judgement than forfeit your favour, which your repeated letters denounce on my refuſal.

I ſend you very little more than the bare occurrences on the ſpot when I took them, and what indigeſted thoughts proceeded from them your own genius and good nature will endeavour to make up and collect their meaning, which my capacity will not permit me to do in as ample a manner as your's may require; I can boaſt of nothing except the bare ſketch or outlines, which want ſuch an artiſt as you to fill up; therefore if you are wearied with its inſipidity, I inſiſt that you attribute it to your own curioſity, that will not be ſatisfied except you know every individual, however trivial.

But now, ſince I mentioned curioſity, you may ſuſpect that I arraign as particular in you what is common to the ſex, on which, if I have made any remarks that may ſeem too ſatyrical, the intent which I aimed it for will in ſome manner excuſe me, becauſe it proceeded from a deſign of reforming what I think is moſt unbecoming in the moſt beautiful of the creation.

What perſon of the leaſt perſpicuity can ſit in a woman's company who affects the refined part of coquetry without noticing it; and what a diſtaſtefull opinion muſt it not produce; and I am apt to believe it creates as much or more contempt in a woman of ſenſe as in a man, who, by a barbarous cuſtom, is obliged ſeemingly to approve with his lips what his heart thoroughly contemns.

The lady mentioned in the latter part of my tour will diſcover that part of the ſpecies which I entirely except againſt; and this is the point alone in which I will feem difobedient, for I will not inform you whether it is a real or a fictitious character.

As to my own country-girls, I will be bold enough to make free with them, and plainly fay any thing without referve ; I fhall not endeavour to apologize if I fomewhere faid they are more given to affectation than thofe with whom I compared them, as I think I need not be afhamed of the comparifon. I read fomewhere that " Affectation is as great an enemy to a pretty face as the fmall-pox ;" but the misfortune of this evil is, it can feldom conceal itfelf for fo long a time as to reap an advantage, but breaks out in fo ungovernable a manner as makes any other quality difagreeable, however good.

I know not by what infatuation that moft of our country women who have been abroad, commonly return home with variety of odd pronunciations, particular geftures, and new fafhions, (perhaps never known in any part of the world, but the production of their own fertile brain, which they impofe upon our credulity as the top of the mode), joined with a contempt of any thing that does not favour of the foreign, and of confequence a general diflike to any of our domeftic commodities; a new plaited cap and tucker,

a reclining of the head, and introducing a new
country-dance, attract the attention more than
the more material part ; an uncommon familiarity
or impudence, with a peculiar accent, compofes
the well-bred woman.

I have remarked more than once, to have feen
one of thefe fafhionable ladies make three court-
feys (to fome acquaintance who juft entered the
front gallery) in repeating the Creed, when the
common ufage of the ceremony required but one ;
fo unreafonably polite are they to make double
the reverence to an acquaintance that they pay
to the Divinity. But what yet gives me much
greater concern is to fee them imitated in their
impertinences by children of not above eight
years old, who never fail of making a better
progrefs in it than they do in their Catechifm :
the maturer part of our ladies do not fo evidently betray their thirft of it as the inexperience
of the young creatures; but whether it would
not be a nobler emulation for them to imitate
examples that would improve the mind, and conduce to a more lafting and folid happinefs than is
to be expected from trifles, is a point, if any of
the practitioners themfelves are afked in a ferious
manner, will allow of. I am quite charmed with
a paper in the Spectator, who fpeaks with fuch

a fpirit as nothing but the juft contempt of thefe inconfiftencies could infpire, and concludes it thus :—" And I defire my fair readers to give a proper direction to their paffion for being admired : in order to which they muft endeavour to make themfelves the objects of a reafonable and lafting admiration. This is not to be hoped for from beauty, or drefs, or fafhion, but from thofe inward ornaments which are not to be defaced by time or ficknefs, and which appear moft amiable to thofe who are moft acquainted with them."

How expreffive is the laft fentence, and what a beautiful idea does it convey of the inward ornaments : they continually difcover fome new perfection, and increafe our efteem for the poffeffor; whereas the more we are acquainted with perfons of the other caft, our efteem gradually leffens, and they betray every day fome latent imperfection. Beauty may pleafe for a while, but to put it in competition with the nobler faculties of the foul would do injuftice to the promoters of permanent happinefs; how often have I juftly feen you admire Juba's fpeech in Cato, where he prefers the inward beauties before the external charms.

" Beauty foon grows familiar to the lover,
Fades in his eye, and palls upon the fenfe;

True fhe is fair (oh, how divinely fair),
But ftill the lovely maid improves her charms,
With inward greatnefs, unaffected wifdom,
And fanctity of manners.''

I have known many inftances of an ugly woman being made agreeable by affability and good-fenfe, but never knew beauty to make an entire conqueft without fome other affiftance; indeed, it may make the firft impreffion, but good-fenfe raifes the pile, and modefty covers it.

You have often urged me to give my fentiments of what I thought would render a woman agreeable in a married ftate, of which I believe there are but few but think lefs or more about it; and as this is the end for which they purpofe themfelves, I think the time but fhort enough to prepare for it, let it be never fo long; and they may take my word they will find it difficult to lay afide any of the airs they have learned young, and the lofs will fit heavy if ever they attempt it; whereas a total ignorance of them will caufe them not to regret what they were unacquainted with, and make them feek enjoyments not to be met with in the giddy world.

I fhall now draw this to a period, and only obferve, you muft not be fcrupuloufly nice in any of my expreffions: I know they will not bear the leaft criticifm, as your impatience did not even allow me time to fettle its order; in return of this my obedience I expect you'll favour me with fome of your productions, fome of which I have already read with the greateft pleafure, and any other which you may hereafter fend me fhall doubly engage the attention of,

Madam,

Your moft obedient,

and moft humble fervant.

JOURNEY THROUGH ENGLAND

IN THE YEAR 1752.

ET fail from Dublin on board the Hibernia, John Morton commander, the eighth day of May, at three o'clock in the afternoon, with a fair wind; the fea to me who was a ftranger, methought it looked exceeding calm. I was enlivened the more as another veffel fet fail the fame tide, and we continued in company fome time, but had foon the mortification to fee them fhoot a head; neverthelefs we ftood out with a fair wind, and at three o'clock next morning (which was Satur-day), got fight of Holy head, and purfued our voyage in fight of Wales. In the evening the wind fhifted, and we were obliged to caft anchor, to wait for the tide, which anfwered the next morning (Sunday) about two o'clock, when we weighed anchor and went by the influence of the tide till we came within three leagues of Liverpool,

which being fpent, we were obliged to the fame
difagreeable work as we had the preceding day ;
I am induced to think that this muft be almoft
the moft difagreeable part of failing, as we are
commonly anxious to arrive at our defired port.
We were obliged to lie here, having no wind
to ftem the tide, but had the pleafing profpect of Wales, which, though fomething moun-
tainous, is as extremely pleafant to one who
thought he fhould never be foon enough at it.
I took this opportunity to refrefh myfelf with
clean linen, the fea having produced fome of the
common effects incident to new failors.

At eight o'clock the king's boat boarded us,
left an officer on board, and went off carrying in
her four of our paffengers, who I fuppofe had the
fame inclination to be out of the wooden world
(as he termed it) as I had. I was fomething difpleafed at the neceffity of ftaying behind, which
was unavoidable, as my father could not go.
Here we lay like a log on the water, and felt a
greater emotion while the veffel was at anchor
than when under fail.

My mufe was interrupted (into which I forgot
to fay I was infenfibly fallen) by our efpying a
boat rowing towards us, which excited my curiofity,
which I foon fatisfied by inquiring of one of the

men, who told me it was another king's boat that belonged to Liverpool ; the head officer and five men again boarded us. I could not help fmiling how eager each was to fearch the fhip, which they did admirably with feveral kinds of tools which they brought for that purpofe.

The officer happening to go into the cabin there found my father, and foon got into converfation with him ; but I need not fay how pleafed I was, when I found he was a Chefhire man, and confequently a countryman of my father's. They foon engroffed the whole converfation to themfelves, and I fo effectually managed the matter, that it was agreed to go afhore in the king's boat. I took fuch things as I fufpected I might have occafion for, if the veffel might be put back by contrary winds, which feemed by its fhifting to anfwer the fufpicion. We put off from the fhip and rowed for about an hour, which brought us within a league of the town, but found ourfelves on the wrong fide of the channel, which obliged us to return round the breakers and prolonged our landing ; this difficulty at length being accomplifhed, we turned down and doubled a point of land called the Red Nofes, which afforded us the profpect of Liverpool, as it is fituate on the fide of a hill adorned with lofty fpires, and makes a moft agreeable landfcape.

I muft confefs, here was I almoft tired with failing, and thought I could never foon enough get foot on Englifh land, as the notions I had entertained of that delightful ifland had filled my mind with fome very venerable thoughts. We fet our fail, the wind fpringing up favoured the option, and in a fmall time we found ourfelves at the fide of the landing-dock.

The Liverpool harbour is accounted dangerous, as there are prodigious fand-banks on either fide the channel, on which if a veffel happens to ftrike, is inevitably loft.

We landed at three o'clock on Sunday evening, and our obliging officer fhowed us to the Lion tavern; when I refted, my head prefented the ceiling dancing, and was fcarce able to make my footing fure; neverthelefs I dreffed in the evening and fallied forth to view the town, which, in my opinion, is very handfome, being compofed chiefly of regular buildings. My female acquaintance, perhaps, may be difpleafed at making any remark before that of the ladies, befides, I fhould be very forry to be found fo unpolifhed, or if you pleafe fo injudicious, when I returned and told 'em I had feen London; therefore I take the liberty to break fomething abruptly from my defcription of Liverpool and its regular buildings to the

more engroffing one of the ladies, who, as I know,
are very curious; yet they muft be content with
general remarks on this head, as I had no
acquaintance, and that they may not be hereafter
furprifed, I fhall make but very few on it, as my
vanity is fuch, I can't fay whether it's a prejudice,
but I fancy my own country girls beyond any I
have feen in Great Britain, and I muft fay that
the women here are in general handfome enough ;
their manners and actions very plain and honeft,
and very apt to credit an improbable ftory ; their
faces befpake this character, as they feem to me
not to have that meaning or vivacity fo common
in Ireland ; they drefs exceeding neat, not complete without the addition of a hat, which no
woman is without, and is, as I may fay, an overgrown fafhion. The better fort drefs extremely
neat, and it fomething furprifed me to find the
refpect they payed here to the Sabbath, whereas
in Ireland it is the day of greateft mirth. I was
directed to a place at the town's end where they
generally walk. This is an agreeable garden,
wherein are three regular plain gravel walks, with
a row of afh trees kept in excellent order ; it is
on a regular defcent, fronted by the fea, which
gives a greater beauty to it, as you may enjoy a
profpect of the veffels as they come in. This

little adventure almoſt tired me, as I had ſlept but
little at ſea ; I thought the beſt ſcheme would
be to return to my lodging, where, when I came,
I wrote two letters, and met with a fellow paſ-
ſenger, who, as he was acquainted beſt with the
cuſtom of the town, he ordered a very good ſupper, confiſting of veal cutlets, pigeons, aſparagus,
lamb and ſalad, apple-pie and tarts. What makes
me ſo particular is, that I was ſurpriſed when I
found the charge ſo extremely reaſonable, I aſſure
you but ſixpence per head, the company confiſting
but of four. I having gained a voracious ſtomach
from the ſea, ſpent little time in diſcourſing, and
after drinking a bottle of port, retired to reſt, and
made one ſleep to Monday, the 11th of May,
when I awoke about eight o'clock. As impatient
as I was to take a further view of the town, I
found another call muſt be ſatisfied firſt, and
accordingly haſted to breakfaſt.

I went firſt to the dock, which was a very
ſpacious one, the entrance of it is guarded by
ſtrong gates. This is joined by another of much
the ſame dimenſions, and both encircle a part of
the town. Here ſhips lie very ſecurely.

I proceeded next to find out my ſhip, which
had arrived the laſt night's tide, as I wanted to
get out my trunk, which I did with ſome difficulty of entry, etc.

Next I went to fee St. Thomas's Church, which is the moſt beautiful piece of modern architecture I had hitherto ſeen ; it is made of freeſtone, adorned with handſome niches, with ſeveral cuts and ſtatues on the outſide ; 'tis of a ſquare figure to the front, but the eaſt end is in a ſemicircle ; the ſteeple or tower of this church is really worth the obſervation of the moſt curious. It is raiſed to a vaſt height, with columns of pillars gradually ariſing out of each other, and are interſperſed with divers cuts and figures ; the windows after the ſame order, with variety of devices. On the top of this is a ſpire (as you would almoſt think) touches the clouds, and ſeems (as it 's made taper-wiſe) as thin as an hair on the top, whereon a neat weather-cock ſtands ; the ſpire is of an octangular form, with beads on every ſquare, and theſe all terminate in a point ; in each ſquare there is a regular window near the top.

I am confident it would tire my friends' patience to give a ſuccinct account of the beauties of this little pile, and I think I hear ſome of 'em cry, " On with the thread of your travels, inform us of the manner of your travelling, what perſons you met, what ſprightly converſation enſued," joined with, " I wonder how you could have the patience to take particular notice of the trifling things in the country, when I was immediately to have the opportunity of feeing London; and befides, what have thofe defcriptions to do with us; it may happen fometime we may have the fame opportunity of feeing thefe things, without your peftering us with the different orders of architecture and fuch like." But hold, my good friends, not fo faft; give me leave to inform you that I did not go to England to fee London alone, of which fo many fine things have been faid, nor merely for the fake of faying, I travelled with fuch and fuch perfons to entertain my acquaintance. I was willing (for the little ftay I made) to know all I could, and for that purpofe took fome few notes on 'em,—this for my own fatisfaction and not as a writer.; therefore, if I commit my little remarks to a friend, I expect he'll as readily accept of the moft trifling as them of a greater confequence; it will be fomething ftrange for me to reaffume St. Thomas's Church, but know, I only gave you a defcription of the outfide, and can't content myfelf without faying fomething of the infide.

I was furprifed to find the feats of this church mahogany, curioufly wrought, all lined with green, the backs carved after the neweft tafte; the pulpit feems to merit a particular defcription; 'tis placed in the middle of a fine marble aifle, the reading-defk under, and the clerk's lower, made of mahogany, with work fuitable to its folemnity, reprefenting King David, Fame, &c., with abundance of other devices ; the top or canopy is hung by a gilded ball from the ceiling, after the manner of two large branches which front it ; the organ-loft and gallery are finely wrought, but plainer. The church is a femicircle, and vaft columns of mahogany (of carved open work) arife, and feem to fupport the great arch above—in a word, 'tis nothing but mahogany carved ; no paint in the whole church.

From thence I proceeded to St. George's Church, built in all refpects like the other, fave the fpire is not fo high, nor is it embellifhed with fo much carvings, and, being old, cuts not fo fine a figure. The other has been modelled from this. The infide is very beautiful, but not fo grand as the other. As I have defcribed it, I think a repetition here of this may feem difagreeable — nay, you may call it ridiculous or impertinent.

I viewed next a church as much remarkable for its age and deformity as the other for the contrary. 'Tis a Gothic building, and, if poffible, ftrikes the mind with awe. The fteeple is not of a remarkable height, is of a fquare form, and has feveral rows of fquare windows after the old fafhion, which makes it appear venerable. There is a fet of bells in this fteeple, which are commonly rung on the arrival of a foreign fhip or a veffel which has been defpaired of. As the church is fituate over the river, the infide of it is divided into four parts, and the gallery in the fame manner; and it's impoffible to take in above half of it in any one view. There are very high windows in it, remarkable for fome panes of ftained glafs.

I am broke off in this part of my defcription, as I think, by fome fimpering or laughing; but, on inquiry, I am furprifed to find it's fome of my female acquaintance, who endeavour to lay the blame on each other. One, of more diftinguifhed vivacity than the reft, feems, by the plaiting of her mouth, willing to fay fomething, and, with mixture of defpite in her tone, thus begins:—

" Never has female refolution been fo much tried. Behold, you've gone on with the dry defcription of three churches. You'd almoft make us fufpect you are an enthufiaft or a bigot—nay, a Methodift never, at his firft appearance on the ftage, hath given us fo high a character of thefe places of worfhip in England."

Why, faith! I forgot the ladies were in company. I beg their pardons, and fhall take care to avoid fuch fuccinct accounts of churches, as I know religion and ladies are things of a different nature.

This little fally of the ladies' wits has fo much put me out of countenance, that I am afraid I fhall not have fpirits enough to go on with my defcriptions. I'faith, I thought of a good expedient to recover 'em, and muft beg the lady's pardon, as it's almoft dinner-time, till I go from the old church to the "Lion" tavern, where an ordinary is kept at one o'clock.

Laft night I gave you a defcription of our fupper, as I could well bear it, becaufe the fea had caufed in me an uncommon appetite, and the recounting of that which gave me infinite pleafure made me fo particular. Now behold me cheerful from all the dainties in feafon and a pint of excellent port, and fit to entertain the ladies with what's moft agreeable. I fhall not trouble 'em with my dinner, only obferve it's accounted one of the beft ordinaries in the kingdom, as you've the niceft and moft uncommon difhes at only eightpence per piece.

The major part of the town (as I hinted already) is furrounded by the two docks. Thefe are kept always in excellent repair, and contain

an incredible quantity of veffels, which are daily
employed by the town. It has within thefe few
years arrived at a very confiderable branch, as
moft of the inland manufactures are exported
from it; they live very neat and regular. They
have almoft finifhed a fine exchange, on which
no expenfe has been fpared, and will be the fineft
in England, except the Royal Exchange in
London.

As the days were now at the longeft, and we
had feen all curious at Liverpool, 'twas agreed to
take a poft-chaife and go to Warrington, about
twelve miles from Liverpool. This we foon executed, and had a pleafant profpect of the country.
'Tis a continued garden all the way. I never
beheld fo delightful a fight; and if any terreftrial
abode can invite, 'tis impoffible this fhould give
place to any. Oh! the fweets difclofed in it are
paft imagination. Behold houfes within a fhot
of each other adorned with beautiful walks and
cut hedges; thefe are common in the pooreft
abode.

The poft-chaife went extremely uneafy, which
made me choofe to take my fervant's horfe, and
give him my place in the chaife; befides, I could
have a more extenfive profpect.

There are a vaft quantity of windmills in this

country. I reckoned in one view fourteen about a mile from Liverpool.

I cannot avoid making a particular remark on one ſmall cottage, which made me ſtay an half an hour behind the chaiſe to behold it. It certainly inſpired me with thoughts ſo pleaſingly romantic that it will give me a pleaſure as often as I think of it. I ſhall fall ſhort of the deſcription of it; not that it's any way remarkable for its building. 'Tis an old pile with three fronts, a croſs on each front; it has two chimneys, and one of 'em ſo artfully covered over with moſs that I at firſt miſtook it for a tree. It certainly makes a pretty figure. Before it ſtands a ſmall garden, contrived after the moſt uſeful manner; it is paled in or incloſed with handſome cut box. There are eleven windows (old faſhion) in the front and nine above. It is ſituate at the top of a delightful verdant hill, and behind it is the ruins of ſeveral old buildings covered with moſs; add to this a number of tall poplar trees, which ſhade and cover the houſe behind, and is made to appear more ſolitary by the croaking of [an] innumerable quantity of rooks who have their habitation in them. In a word, 'tis ſo amazingly ſtriking that I was quite loſt in ecſtaſy, and never conſidered how far my company was gone. Neceſſity

at length prevailed on my unwillingnefs, and I
went off juft as I ended this foliloquy :—

"Oh! thou lovely abode; how much more
preferable art thou to all the gaudy fhows of
grandeur! Thou exciteft venerable thoughts, and
appeareft yet more lovely the longer we know
thee. How ferenely contented could I pafs my
life with thee, and defpife all the fopperies, if my
other wifhes correfponded with that of thy manfion! But, ah! thou art referved for fome more
happy one that can ufe thee beft as thou deferveft,
and in tranquillity behold thy beauties. Adieu,
thou lovely place, let thy affiftance heighten the
. blifs of one that can in peace poffefs thee!"

From this romantic ftrain it may be fufpected
I had read the "Economy of Human Life." The
ladies may conjecture, by the agitation I feemed
to be in, that I was in love, and perhaps defpifed,
and may probably conjecture 'twas that which
made 'em experience fome of the effects of it in
fome of the foregoing fentences; as there hath
been inftances wherein the whole fex hath fuffered from a particular prejudice, it would be
impoffible for me to prevent people's fufpicions,
but I can affure 'em 'tis nothing of all that. It
may feem fomething furprifing that I cannot
rightly account for it myfelf. I believe it's owing

to the different objects which ſtrike the mind, and I really believe mine is a medley of all kinds; and in ſome particular times you may ſee me cry and laugh by intervals.

If this cannot avail me, I muſt contentedly ſubmit to the cenſure; but I cannot help ſmiling when I think hereafter I ſhall give the moſt exalted praiſe to the condemning ſex. If the female one ſuſpects I here mean them, I cannot prevent their thinking 'ſo, more than I can that of my being in love.

This digreſſion brings me after a ſmart trot up with my company, who I obſerved before had got the ſtart of me, and found 'em ſtopped about a half a mile's diſtance from the little happy retreat, at a decent houſe, enjoying themſelves at the door (for they did not alight) with cups of fine ale, here preferable to the richeſt wine. I drank of it as it pleaſed my taſte, and I had almoſt inſenſibly loſt thoſe romantic ideas which had engroſſed my thoughts. Here, then, is a proof of my variable temper.

I ſhould have told who my company were ſooner, but, as they had no relation with my preceding narrative, thought it might as opportunely fall in in another place. They conſiſted but of two, viz., my father, the gay Valerius, and

myfelf, and you may include the fervant, if you
think he was a fquire good enough for fuch a
hero as I.

I hinted before I had given my place in the
chaife to the fervant, but then I forgot to tell
you what Valerius did, why he mounted the
fecond horfe, which my father rode, becaufe he
chofe the feat.

Valerius and I rode in company through the
delightful country till we came to Warrington,
which was about feven in the evening. The
roads are the moft difagreeable part of it, as they
are very deep.

This town is clean, handfome enough, and
regular. The bulk of it is in one large ftreet.
We found everything abounding here in plenty.
We ordered an agreeable collation, and went to
reft about ten.

Sol had no fooner fhot his firft rays but they
apprifed me of his approach. I hafted from my
bed, as I was impatient to behold the country
which ravifhed my fenfes fo much the day before.
For that purpofe I mounted to the higheft room
in the houfe, and directed my eyes over a vaft
plain diverfified with fweeteft colours from the
influence of the fun, who in oblique rays emitted
a feeble warmth more pleafing than in mid-day.

I believe I fhould have remained in this pofture fomething longer, had not the tinkling of the tea-fpoons againft the difhes (which I muft needs fay the waiter ftruck with fome vehemence, as I heard 'em in the room under as he laid breakfaft) reminded me 'twas as neceffary to pleafe fome other fenfe befides that of feeing, and for that purpofe hurried down, where I found my father and Valerius over a piece of toaft, who laughed at my entrance. I immediately underftood their meaning, as I found they were willing to deprive me of my fhare.

Here our tour had almoft been delayed by an unforefeen accident; that having inquired for our poft-chaife, the man refufed letting it go farther without an additional price, as he found we could not immediately get horfes: we infifted on our agreement with the owner fome time to no pur-pofe, till, threatening him with the juftice and adding to it a tankard of ale, we at length pre-vailed. This was a man who had been fent to affift the boy to take back the cattle; this was an open villany, which I am afraid is too much practifed and too little taken notice of in Eng-land.

I would not be underftood here to caft this as a reflection on the whole country, as none is free

from vitiated perfons, but in part to take off fome
of the odium generally thrown on ours; and
were we impartially to confider matters, we
might find we are not even as much addicted to
thofe vices as they who would rid themfelves of
'em at our expenfe.   But to return: we fet out
in our poft-chaife, Valerius and the fervant rid as
before; we had not gone a mile when we were
obliged to relinquifh it and exchange places with
the two horfemen.   In all the world I believe
there are not fuch roads as thefe, they being but
a continued heap of ridges, fo very deep that I
expected every minute when I fhould be fwallowed
up in fome of 'em.   We fuffered three over-
turnings before we could perfuade ourfelves to
quit our vehicle; the poor horfes were to be
pitied, for one or the other was feldom five
minutes on his legs.

With much difficulty we at length arrived at
Knutsford about one o'clock, and were directed
to the Swan Inn, a very fine one; here we dined
on variety of difhes at a very moderate expenfe.
This is but a fmall town, though handfome
enough; it is very dead, not having any particular trade to enliven it except fome thread-
makers, and them but a few.

I never beheld fo fweet a profpect as faluted

mine eyes all the way, it being but an extenfive garden ; not one place is ufelefs or become vacant ; the print of the induſtrious hufbandman is to be feen on every fide, and betrays the vigilance of its inhabitants, 'tis mighty rare to find any hand unemployed.

" Ignavum Fucos Pecus à Præfepibus arcent."

Virg. [*Georg.* iv.]

Oh ! how it elates the heart to behold all thofe things in their increafing nature, and to fee how the hufbandman expects to be rewarded for his pains ! Who then would not feek for fuch a one when fuch ample amends at laſt crowns the labour ?

Dinner being over, we purfued our journey in the fame order as before related through this delightful elyfium : the harveſt now advancing gave us an opportunity to find Ceres on her part had not been flothful, but had fpread her induftrious hand over moſt part of it.

The frequent overturning of our chaife obliged us often to turn back to give Valerius and the fervant affiftance ; as the chaife could come on but flowly, my father and I agreed to go on fomething fafter, which we put in execution till we arrived within a half-a-mile of town, where we intended to take up our lodgings ; here was fome

excellent ale, with which we refreſhed ourſelves.
This put in my head a piece of humour which I
thus managed :—

I told the man of the houſe that we were
obliged to quit our poſt-chaiſe becauſe of the bad
roads, and that we exchanged with our ſervants,
who followed us in it ; that as ſoon as he ſaw it he
ſhould order 'em to haſten, and withal give 'em
a pint of ale, which I then paid him for.   I
knew this would take, as the ſervant had a livery
on who rode with Valerius.

We rode on, and it may be ſuſpected I was not
a little pleaſed at my ſcheme, though I did not
impart it to my father, who, having occaſion to
alight, ſaid he would go into town in the chaiſe.
I was much pleaſed at the propoſal, as it ſoon
would reſolve me of the event of my project,
which ſucceeded according to the intent I had
propoſed ; for on Valerius's approach he aſked
me what put it in my noddle to order a pint
of ale for him by that unmannerly man, who deſired him to haſten after the gentlemen.   I made
no reply but a ſmile, aſking him would he exchange places, which he readily complying, we
ſoon ſeated ourſelves, and in that manner arrived
in leſs than a half an hour at Macclesfield.

It was about ſeven o'clock when we arrived at

the town, and having been fatigued much the two preceding days, thought the moſt prudent ſcheme would be to defer any curioſity till the next day, and only for the preſent order ſomething light and agreeable for ſupper, and retire to reſt. This motion was ſeconded by Valerius, who crept into the larder and brought with him a brace of fine pullets, which were immediately ordered to the fire, and in leſs than an hour found 'em in that order we had deſired 'em.

At my ſetting out from Cork I had appointed a particular friend to advertiſe me of any news he thought I would be deſirous of knowing; the foot he and I had always lived upon, and the probity I knew him endued with that made me regard him rather as a brother. I had but one letter from him ſince my departure, and that was three weeks, which ſomething ſurpriſed me, as I had wrote to him almoſt every poſt, giving him a ſuccinct account of what related to myſelf, and what elſe I ſuſpected might be agreeable to him. I did not account this neglect to anything, except he might conjecture I was ſo taken up as not to admit any time for the peruſal or anſwering his; but then it occurred that as I had wrote ſo often it could not be the caſe: as it was im-poſſible to form any probable notion of it, I fufpended all fufpicions till I could have a plainer proof.

I thought thus much neceffary to premife, as I may have fome occafion hereafter to fpeak of him ; fo that if this digreffion is not altogether fo entertaining, yet it may be not altogether un-ufeful.

After the cloth was removed, we ftayed not long to chat; I caft myfelf into the arms of Somnus, and buried all my thoughts in a pro-found fleep, and believe I made but an entire fleep of the whole night ; I awoke not till eight the next morning, the 13th of May. At break-faft I met with fomething unthought of, namely, a very genteel girl about eighteen, who prefided at the tea-table ; fhe feemed to me to be well verfed in what is called (now-a-days) politenefs, for fhe received me with an air fuitable to the profeffors of it.

Our converfation turned upon indifferent topics, and found fhe was but lately come from London, where fhe had been for upwards of a year with a fifter who lived there. This eafed all my doubts concerning her, for when I had an opportunity, I inquired and found fhe was our landlord's daughter. I endeavoured to correct the brogue natural to our country, and told her I believed

the manners of the country but ill correfponded
with the refined ones fhe lately had feen in
London ; for my part, as I was an entire ftranger,
and was going there, fome little inftruction from
her would be of more weight and have greater
efficacy on my mind than double the number
from any other perfon.

This obliging difcourfe made her fmile, as I
endeavoured to accompany it with ferioufnefs ;
but on obferving I expected an anfwer, fhe replied, " That however miftaken fome people may
be in their notions, the country fometimes afforded
politenefs little inferior to that of the town ; the
laft example fhe had of it from me convincing
her of the truth of what fhe before fufpected."

I found the lady was not to be impofed on
entirely, and that there required a little more
acquaintance to make her believe the fincerity of
what I urged, and found I was caught in the fame
trap ; for I perceived fhe alfo expected an anfwer,
which was, " that I fhould always acknowledge
the penetration of a lady's judgment, efpecially
hers who was obliging enough to fave the blufhes
of the ignorant, by friendly attributing to 'em
accomplifhments which they never were fenfible
of being poffeffed of."

After a few compliments naturally arifing on

this head, we parted. I went to my chamber to drefs, and perhaps fhe might have done the fame, but my curiofity being excited after a more peculiar manner, I heeded not the trifle of her dreffing or any other employment which may at that juncture engrofs her time. When I was in my chamber and alone, I had then an opportunity of indulging fome reflections on this little adventure.

On my firft meeting with her I thought fomething ftruck me more than is ordinary for girls of her condition to infpire; fhe feemed to have all that delicacy and unaffectednefs requifite to perfons of the firft rank, without betraying any of that awkwardnefs or timidity common to a low ftation. I faw fhe had wit, accompanied with a competency of judgment, and a vivacity or fprightlinefs which feldom fails of being agreeable. As to her perfon, fhe was rather low of the two extremes, and as fhe was naturally fat, it rather diminifhed than added to her ftature. Her face was not what is accounted beautiful, but had a foftnefs or fweetnefs which denoted an agreement of temper. A good fet of teeth and a pair of penetrating grey eyes was no fmall addition; fo that, upon the whole, I thought fhe was to be admired rather than treated after the manner of one of an equal condition; and in all probability her father could have given a fortune to her which would render her not deſpicable.

As ſuch, then, ſhe ſtood in my opinion; ſo that I reſolved to treat her agreeable to it. I cannot ſay what it was, but I really had a deſire to be again in her company: it did not ſeem the leaſt like love, but ſomething unaccountable I never obſerved in myſelf before.

Theſe different agitations delayed my dreſſing ſomething longer than uſual, ſo that, on my coming down, on inquiry, [I] found Miſs Dama (for that was her name) was gone to church. I was ſomething diſpleaſed, but Valerius happening to meet me, aſked if I would not view the town; and I replying in the affirmative, we immediately went out. We walked over ſome of the ſtreets, which were exceeding clean; but of this hereafter. On the turning of one of 'em I thought I heard a bell ring, and, on paſſing through a ſmall lane, I found myſelf at a church, for it ſeemed the people had not as yet gone in. I propoſed to Valerius going to church, as I ſuſpected we ſhould there find Dama; beſides, I ſhould have the opportunity of ſeeing it. I looked all round during divine ſervice, but could not ſee her; till I at length grew weary of it,

F

and concluded fhe had not come thither. After
it was done, I procured the fexton to fhow us the
church. 'Tis a large old ftructure ; all the pews
are made of oak, nothing elfe being remarkable
in it, except an old ftone erected in one fide of
it to the memory of Sir Richard Legh of Lyme,
now fucceeded by his great-grandfon, who lives
in the manfion houfe of the family near this
town ; and for curiofity [I] have taken a copy
as it is in the old characters :—

> " Here Lyethe the bodie of Perkin a Legh,
> That for king Richard the death did die,
> Betrayed for righteovfnes :
> And the bones of Sir Peers his fone,
> That with King Henrie the fift did wonne,
> in Paris.
> This Perkin ferved king Edward the Third and the Black
> Prince his Sonne in all their warres in France, and was
> at the battell of Creffie, and hadd Lyme given him for that
> fervice, and after their deathes ferved king Richard the
> Second, and left him not in his troubles, but was taken with
> him, and beheaded at Chefter by king Henrie the Fourth ;
> and the fayd fir Peers his fonne ferved king Henrie the
> Fift and was flaine at the battell of Agincourt.   In their
> memorie fir Peter Legh of Lyme knight defcended from
> them, fynding the faid ould Verfes written upon a ftone
> in this chapel did re-edifie this Place An°. Dom . 1620." [1]

From hence I entered on the left fide of the
church to a very old fquare area, called Earl

[1] Collated with Ormerod, iii. 367.

Rivers' Chapel, whoſe family are all interred here.
There are four monuments in it, a man and a
woman in each, being the predeceſſors of ſaid
family. The oldeſt of theſe monuments is upwards of four hundred years. The lateſt or laſt
earl is but a ſingle man cut in marble, and moſt
exquiſitely wrought, leaning on a cuſhion, holding
one of his hands open as if willing to graſp.

His ſon Robert, the preſent earl (as they ſay),
in his juvenile days, being profligate, broke his
father's eſcritoir, and took thence fifteen hundred
pounds to ſupport his extravagance. The old
man was much vexed, and endeavoured to hang
him, but his majeſty, conſidering his avarice,
pardoned him.

Upon his deceaſe the ſon declared he would
place him in a poſture ſuitable to his avarice,
by putting him in a manner of endeavouring to
gripe at all, in which way he is as above related.
This piece coſt upwards of a thouſand pounds.

This chapel was founded four hundred years
ago by the Archbiſhop of York, who took ſuch
a liking to it, that he ordered his heart to be
interred here, which, when he died, was accordingly executed, and the figure of it is cut an-
tiquely on the ſtone under which it was buried,
but is now ſo worn by the continual treading on

it as it is fcarce difcernible, except the bare figure.

In one corner of this place is a ftone which a woman purchafed of the Pope as a pardon for herfelf and fix children for one thoufand years. The fexton makes confiderably by this ftone, as he has found a method of taking the impreffion on a large fheet of paper, one of which I now have. There are fome old characters at the bottom, not intelligible by any one I could as yet find.

The outfide of this church makes a Gothic appearance. The fteeple is low, hath fix indiffe-rent bells, and chimes the Fourth Pfalm. 'Tis placed on a very fteep hill, under which runs a very agreeable river, which adds to the mufic of the bells. The yard of the church is kept in good repair, and near it is a poor houfe or public fchool, where children are taught to work, read, write, &c.

The forenoon being pretty well taken up with viewing thofe things, we difcharged the fexton, Valerius chiding at the fame time my too parti-cular curiofity, as he called it.

We returned to our inn, and had the pleafure to find things in forwardnefs for dinner. I could not as yet put Dama out of my head, who, as I

was informed, was but juſt come in. I aſked no
further queſtions concerning her. Valerius took
up a newſpaper which he ſaw lie on the table;
and when I found he was engaged in it, I took the
opportunity of retiring. I went immediately into
my own chamber, adjoining to another room,
which as I paſſed by, [I] peeped in the key-hole,
where I ſaw Dama reading. I did not ſtay long
in my room, but returned haſtily, as if I only
wanted ſomething. As I knew the room ſhe was
in [was] free to any, I made no ceremony of entering, at which ſhe ſhut the book and laid it
on the table; on obſerving which, I ſaid I hoped
I had not intruded on her meditations. She
replied, with a careleſs air, "that the ſubject ſhe
had been engaged on required not ſuch deep attention as to put me under the neceſſity of an
apology; that ſhe had taken up that merely to
kill the time between dinner."

"Whatever has," ſaid I, "the luck to contri-
bute to your diverſion cannot, I am ſure, fail of
making any one curious; and as this ſeems to be
in print," added I, taking it up, "I fancy it is
no ſecret; therefore, to let me ſhare with you
the pleaſure will add more to the obligations
I already have held from you."

"The obligations," replied ſhe, "you ſeem to

hint you've received from me have not as yet
come within my knowledge, and therefore I ſhall
diſpenſe with any return until they do ; as I am
convinced of my giving no room for thanks,
[it] makes me ſuſpect I ſhall wait ſome time for
the performance."

I then opened the book, and found it a novel
tranſlated from the French ; upon which I cried,
ſomething maliciouſly, " Oh, Madam ! I perceive
there are obligations of a different kind than
what I experienced, holden from you, which, I
believe, you'll not acknowledge as ſuch."

Upon which ſhe replied, looking ſomething
tenderly, " That we gentlemen ſuſpected every
one had as good an opinion of our excellencies
as ourſelves."

I anſwered that " I was ſenſible there were but
too many coxcombs with a great deal of vanity
and little judgment that ſeemed to have the
opinion ſhe ſpoke of; but I knew her capacity
too well to think her judgment would permit her
to place her affections on one of them ; that
I hoped ſhe would find perſons of merit, even
in our ſex, one of which, I doubted not, was
her choice."

She anſwered, with ſomething of a free and
gay voice, " That ſhe muſt beg a truce, as all

her ſtore of compliments were exhauſted ; that I had choſen a very ſilly topic to beſtow 'em on, who was not capable of making a ſuitable return ; that I muſt not account it impertinent in her if ſhe deſired I ſhould drop the point hitherto diſputed."

This pleaſed me much, as I had almoſt found myſelf in the ſame dilemma ; and, beſides, ſhe gave me an opportunity of turning the converſation to the point I aimed at.

" I am glad," reſumed I, " you put it in my power to ſhow, by this ſmall mark of compliance, my readineſs in obeying any of greater moment. I, who am now a ſtranger here, ſhould be much indebted to you for the trouble of ſhowing me any curioſity this town affords."

After ſhe had muſed a while, ſhe replied that ſhe knew of none in town except ſome agreeable walks, which ſhe would ſhow me another time ; but if I could undertake to walk about a mile and a half off to a ſmall town called Preſtbury, where there were ſome old buildings, and an organ in the church, " which," added ſhe, " if you've an inclination to ſee, I am acquainted with the organiſt ; and I ſhall get a couple of other young ladies, which, with your friend, will, I flatter myſelf, not altogether make a diſagreeable troop."

This obliging propofal exactly correfponded with the fcheme I before had laid in my own imagination. I received it with all the refpect and politenefs I was capable of. We were dif-courfing of it when a fervant entered, and put an end to our *tête-a-tête* converfation by in-forming us that dinner waited.

On entering the parlour, I found Valerius chewing a cruft of bread, who told me that I had delayed his dinner near five minutes, and begged I would[1] fit down, for which purpofe he had drawn a chair. Dama entering a little after, caufed fome other compliments on the occafion.

When I found my ftomach permitted, I opened the fcheme to Valerius, who feemed very glad of it. "Befides," added he, "I can jangle the organ a little, which, if it happens to pleafe the ladies, [I] fhall account myfelf happy."

My father relifhed it alfo, and faid he would ride fo far to be a partaker. We agreed to leave the management of it to Dama, who faid fhe thought it beft to do it early next morning, as it would require fome time to prepare her friends and the organift.

Matters being thus adjufted, Dama faid fhe'd go to make her vifits. Valerius and I went to

' MS. reads *may.*

my chamber, where, after remaining fome while, I thought it beft to take another walk about the town. As I came downftairs my father met me, and told me he had procured a friend to fhow us a curiofity. As the time lay on our hands, we readily agreed; whereupon there was a decent-looking man introduced to us. He feemed to be of the ignorant, honeft caft, and feemed ready to oblige us.

We did not appear anxious to know whither he intended fhowing us, till Valerius inquired, when he informed us 'twas the filk mills. As I had heard a character of 'em, I was the better pleafed.

As we went on, I faid to Valerius I was forry we had not Dama with us. Our conductor, hearing her name, turned and afked me what I thought of her. I replied, I thought fhe was an agreeable girl. He faid, nodding his head, " So it might hap. For his part, he knew nothing on her, but heard fome of the folks fay fhe had learned a great many fine airs lately in London; and her father would have been e'en as well pleafed had fhe ftayed at home; for," added he, " they fay her feather and fhe hath quarrelled about it, and faid he was afraid fhe had learned no good there; whereupon fhe threatened to go

G

back again. That's all, meafter," quoth the fellow, " I know on't. 'Tis not my bufinefs to interfere in't, I only feay what other folks fay."

This, joined with the fimplicity he expreffed it with, ferved to convince me there was fomething extraordinary in the gay appearance this fair lady made, and to confirm fome fufpicions I entertained from the fecond time of my converfing with her. I made the man no reply, but that it concerned me as little as it did himfelf, and did not trouble myfelf about it.

Though I might have had fome few conjectures at this time concerning this affair, I fhall omit explaining 'em here till I have more leifure, but tell you by this time I am arrived at the filk mills, the defcription of which I fhall fall fhort in, but as I guefs I have excited the curiofity of my friends concerning this furprifing machine, I fhall attempt it in the beft manner I can.

I firft entered the ground floor, where I faw three vaft engines compofed of about eight hundred bobbins each, which fpin the filk as it comes raw from India. From hence I afcended the fecond loft, where I faw one thoufand nine hundred bobbins turned by the fame wheel, winding the filk on fwifts, which is fpun on the

lower engines; and on the upper or laſt floor
are ſeveral new machines as experiments for the
improvement of the aforeſaid work.

This grand piece of mechaniſm coſt upwards
of ten thouſand pounds, and was a conſiderable
time in building. The workmanſhip is really
admirable, as ſmall ſticks not as thick as a hair
do their reſpective duties with the utmoſt ex-
actneſs, and without intermiſſion. This variety
put in my mind the words of Portius in Mr.
Addiſon's excellent tragedy of Cato :—

" Nor ſees with how much art the windings run,
Nor where the regular confuſion ends."

I could, I believe, have ſtayed weeks to behold this huge engine, and find ſome beauty or
curioſity I had not before perceived. I cannot
in any reſpect convey an idea of ‚it to one who
hath not ſeen it, but make 'em to faintly admire
this exceſſive piece of art, which I thought could
not be performed by man.

Having ſpent beſt part of this day in walking
and other amuſements, about ſix I thought I
had a propenſion for ſleeping, and accordingly
haſtened to my chamber, where I threw myſelf
on my bed, and was ſurpriſed when I could not
ſleep. Thoughts of various kinds filled my
brain, which of confequence draw reflections;

among the number of which I happened to hit
on what our guide to the mills had, as I thought,
undefignedly fpoken concerning Dama; after
weighing the manner he expreffed it, I concluded
I had fome reafon to ground a fufpicion of her
having learned fome of the airs *à la mode* lately
in London. This entirely banifhed any thoughts
concerning her, and as I found fleep would not
befriend me, I aroufed myfelf and took a book
I faw in the window. I was not an half [hour]
reading, when the door flew open, and prefented
Dama, who run up immediately, and told
me fhe had got the organift, who [1] now waited
below to have the pleafure of being introduced
to me. I faid no more but that I was at her
command, and followed her down. On entering
the parlour I faw in appearance a genteel man,
who[2] very politely told me he would accompany
us to the church. Valerius coming in foon after
repeated the fame ceremony I had gone through
before, but I muft confefs it was done with a
greater air of politenefs, as it was attended
with a multiplicity of bows, fome of which had
almoft coft him a fall on a couple of young
ladies entering, who were to be of the party.
I endeavoured to exert myfelf after the example

---

[1] MS. has *and who.*　　　[2] MS. has *and.*

of Valerius, but not with half his ſuccefs, for
after I was done I found he had reſerved a
ſuperior ſalute for the ladies, for he not only
kiſſed his hand, but ſcraped too with that violence as entirely tore a piece off his ſhoe, which
I am apt to conjecture was before broke by the
frequent uſe of this polite exerciſe.

It may be ſuppoſed that we all readily agreed
to the little excurſion propoſed by Dama, and
accordingly 'twas reſolved to ſet out about eight
next morning on foot, as we could the better
enjoy ourſelves than if we rode, and for that purpoſe had appointed this room for the place of
rendezvous, when Dama promiſed to have
breakfaſt ready. We talked on the pleaſure we
ſhould have next day, and Valerius, looking
tenderly on one of the ladies, ſaid he would
petition for a fine day, which he doubted not of
obtaining on ſo divine a cauſe, and as he had
more than once performed a part in a play, he
very gracefully repeated ſome ſpeeches *à propos ;*
after Valerius [had] received ſome compliments
but the due of his merits, we retired to our
reſpective apartments, though I might have had
Dama's company longer.

I was arouſed next morning about ſeven by an
unexpected ſpeech of Valerius, who lay in the

next bed to me, who cried out with an unuſual vociferation—

"The great, th' important day."

As he ſtarted me ſomething, I replied haſtily that an hour's ſleep would be of more importance to me than his damned nonſenſe. Neverthelefs, I conſidered the time was but barely neceſſary to prepare myſelf, and accordingly I honoured the " great, important day" by riſing quickly.

Our little aſſembly ſoon met, and when break-faſt was over, we purſued our journey which was rendered very agreeable by the frequent witticiſms of Valerius, which he very judiciouſly knew how to adapt to the occaſion, and got to Preſtbury when I thought we were not half way ; but the miles in this part of the country are ſo ſmall, that you may inſenſibly paſs over a number of them.

This town, though ſmall, is extremely agreeable ; it is but one long regular ſtreet, which, as it is encompaſſed by many orchards and well-improved meadows, appears very inviting.

We proceeded to the church, which looks as ancient as time, being built of limeſtone, cut with various devices and croſſes after the old method ; the ſteeple or tower is very romantic, in which are ſix ſmall bells. The inſide of this church is

of very old oak, and pictures of the twelve
Apoftles are againft each pillar. The pulpit was
hung in mourning for the death of Sir William
Meredith and his lady, who both died about fix
months before. The organ to the front makes a
pretty appearance, but difappoints your opinion
of its goodnefs when you come to play on it, as it
makes a very fqueaking noife.

When we were fufficiently fatisfied with the
church, Valerius protefted he could not walk back
to dinner until he had taken a wet, as he called
it : and as he is one of the moft active men in
thofe cafes, he went into a tavern (there being an
excellent one in this town), and produced fome
cold roaft beef, Chefhire cheefe, and a cool tankard, which was very agreeable to the weather,
ftrongly recommending the ladies to his treat. I
muft confefs none of us turned his fubject into
ridicule, for we eat heartily.

I forgot to mention we had engaged the organift
to dine with us, and when we were on our return,
he fent one to tell us he ought to be remembered
for his trouble. We then fent him a half-a-crown,
withal telling him we did not defire his company
at dinner. I never faw fo mercenary a fellow.
His name was Ridley.

This furnifhed us with matter fufficient to

entertain us longer than the time we could take
to return to dinner, which was in about an hour
after, where we found a very good one prepared ;
but the heat of the day and Valerius his treat
prevented me from eating much here. We had
fcarce done, when we were alarmed by the ringing
of bells, and were informed it 'twas for us, but
in the evening were convinced of it, when the
body of ringers came to us, who, after we had
difcharged [them], rung moft part of the night.

After dinner my father went to take a view of
the town, [in] which, as I was tired, [I] could not
accompany him ; but Valerius, whofe fpirits were
feldom flack, faid he would. I refrefhed myfelf
by a nod, and Dama, returning afterwards, afked
me if I would accompany her in a little walk. I
made no hefitation, but accepted it. Neverthelefs, I was fomething difpleafed, as I had partly
made an engagement with a friend of my father's
for this evening.

The ferenity of the day invited us to walk
further than at firft propofed, and certainly the
innumerable improvements which furround this
place would ravifh any mortal whofe fenfes were
not entirely funk into ftupidity. Thus drawn,
we infenfibly walked until we found ourfelves at
a foot of a moft delicious mountain, overfpread

with all the rural delights; a murmuring rivulet added freſh beauty to it, when on the declivity of the oppoſite hill a handſome houſe feaſted our eyes with all its gardens and water-works; the harmleſs flock ſkipped and played, and by their bleating (in innocence enjoying[1] themſelves) ſeemed quite happy in this heavenly place; the feathered race on their part were no leſs aſſiduous, and by their endeavours, though little, added great delight to it; the meandering ſtream, as conſcious of its ability, ſeemed to diſplay its[2] higheſt notes, and quavering lulled in ecſtaſy the ſoul; the little ſun-flies ſeem[ed] delighted and "gilded" ſport amongſt themſelves on the ſurface. I quite tranſported lay, gazing on the verdant beauties now all in bloom, when Dama minded [me] 'twas now grown late and time to ſhelter; I begged her to let me enjoy myſelf a little longer and entreated her to go to the top of the hill to have a more extenſive proſpect; when I was ſeated under the branches of a lofty oak, no knight-errant could be filled with more romantic notions. I fancied I was ſome exiled prince and my prin-ceſs was partaking of my misfortunes; at ſome times I was ſo timorous of diſpleaſing her that I would ſcarce touch her, and I doubt not but

---

[1] MS. has *enjoyed.*   [2] MS. has *her.*

I anfwered her, "my princefs," or after fome fuch manner.

Though the remotenefs of the place and the familiarity fhe admitted me to may give room to fome fufpicions not entirely to her advantage, yet the refpect I bore my princefs at that juncture may in fome meafure invalidate it; neverthelefs, after having remained fo long and being con-fcious of an opinion which might[1] prevail, fhe grew fomeway peevifh; whether or no fhe might[2] fufpect her virtue was in danger or any other motive, I fhall not pretend to fay, but leave that to the judicious to determine.

I endeavoured to fatisfy her in what I thought affected her; I exclaimed againft the wilful follies of youth, told her how [the] different fexes may en-joy each other, foothe and make gentle [love?] in the utmoft innocence, applauded and extolled pla-tonics to the fkies; whether this was the way of pleafing and giving her a good opinion of me or not, I fhall leave to be determined with the former.

I led my Statira back, who, as we had walked pretty faft, was fomething fatigued, fo that I had not the pleafure of feeing her the reft of the day; my father and Valerius returning from their ramble, they entertained me with a detail of their adventures.

---

[1] MS. has *may.*   [2] *Idem.*

Next morning my father propofed vifiting an old acquaintance of my grandfather's, and for that purpofe provided a couple of horfes, and after a mile's ride [we] found ourfelves at a very neat houfe. We were immediately introduced to him, and as time had left his marks on him in fo particular a manner, a defcription of him may not altogether feem improper.

He is about ninety-fix, and his looks, though not auftere, yet [are] not tinctured with any of that effeminacy fo common to age, and in fome refpect draw veneration; his gray locks hung gracefully on his fhoulders, and while he ftood erect as a man of twenty, he feemed buried in contemplation; when he took notice of me he afked me divers queftions, which, if I fhould here repeat, [I] may feem to run too far into particulars.

From hence we proceeded to vifit a man of eighty-four, and were directed to a very pleafant vale, where his houfe was fituate upon a brook. Here we found the old man, who feemed very fprightly; he was not fo grave or folid as the firft, but, on the contrary, was all alacrity, mirth, and facetioufnefs. He told many diverting ftories, and very frankly gave us a tune of his violin. As I remembered of an engagement with one Mrs. Gill, I haftened homewards to put myfelf in a condition of fulfilling it.

Accordingly, at the appointed hour, I appeared
at Mrs. Gill's, who received me with a good deal
of politenefs. I had got the ftart of fome ladies,
who fhe told me had engaged themfelves with
her that evening. This, as it was unexpeĉted,
pleafed me. I had forgot to fay Valerius was
with me.

Not long after two of the ladies came. Valerius difplayed all the *congees* he was mafter of,
and as he is a man who naturally hates circum-
locution, moft of his compliments commonly con-
fift in fcrapes. Thefe ladies were hardly placed,
when three more immediately followed, which
increafed our number to five. I found it would
require more time than I could well fpare to make
a particular acquaintance with any of them ; therefore I thought general converfation fitter for the
occafion. Two of'em were handfome, and perhaps
the other three might feem fo to another perfon.
I found ne'er a wit amongft them (a kind of an
animal I deteft), neither could I difcern the leaft
tinĉture of the prude or coquet. Any one may
fuppofe that our prattle was unmixed with any of
the reigning diftempers in Ireland, where a girl
thinks fhe cannot fhew herfelf to advantage without being miftrefs of fome of thefe neceffary quali-
fications. I alfo apprehend that a little pride is

feldom wanting to fome of our ladies, who I am perfuaded would make as good, nay, a better figure without it, for as it is commonly productive of vanity, vanity gives 'em too great an opinion of any little excellency they are miftrefs[es] of, and by that means obfcure[s] its beauty, which perhaps may redound to their praife and inward fatiffaction, if it was not accompanied with too high an opinion of its value.

How we came to have this reflection caft upon us by the Englifh, well known by the name of Irifh pride, I fhall not anfwer; but then I am induced to think that it muft have arifen from facts, and as the appellation is general to the country, fo I fuppofe the facts which produced it muft alfo be neceffarily general.

If my young miffes will not pardon this digreffion, their vanity may give them that fatiffaction my pen cannot; neverthelefs I muft affure them 'tis with difpleafure I have obferved it fo univerfally practifed, neither would I have 'em think but I have their welfare more at heart than that of our neighbouring ladies. Everybody, even a coquet, will allow with me that though the fprightly airs, affected poftures, lifping, and all its train of impertinences, that though, I fay, they feldom fail of pleafing, yet fhew me even the wildeſt rake, or one man out of an hundred, that would not chooſe (were he to marry) the unaffected, plain-dealing, and goodnatured woman. Were I not zealous for their intereſts, I ſhould not have ſtept ſo far out of my road to give 'em this word of advice; as this is not intended for the preſs, ſo it cannot reach all our Iriſh ladies; therefore I only intend it for ſuch of my acquaintance as I regard, and who I ſhould be glad would reform if they are troubled with this diſorder.

Though it was with ſatisfaction I partook of theſe ladies' converſation, yet I could not avoid regretting ſo viſible a want of it in ours, as ſincerity with us is not commonly a concomitant of the tea-table; here then I thought it viſible on every feature, but if it can be any pleaſure to the fair in this kingdom, I can tell 'em 'tis not a general practice all over England, for I found the ſcene entirely altered when I came to London, though my ſtay was ſo ſhort.

I am convinced of a failing I have (if it can be termed ſuch), and though I know the folly on't, yet for my life I can't break myſelf of it; I am generally baſhful, or in other words which I think more proper, timid in a ſtrange company, and it muſt be ſome time that can bring me to

exprefs myfelf freely; I can't fay by what means
it[1] forfook me in this agreeable company, and I
could as freely converfe with any of 'em in lefs
than a half an hour as with my clofeft acquaintance. I mention this one circumftance barely to
demonftrate how fincerity alone can make a lafting
friendfhip, and it fhould be from this principle
we fhould judge how we may depend on a readinefs of being ferved.

Without farther comments upon this head
I fhall difmifs it, as I fhall likewife the tea-table
and our enfuing difcourfe, of which I was forry
to deprive myfelf fo fuddenly, which the neceffity
of writing a couple of letters compelled me to;
after I had finifhed them, I partook of a light .
repaft and foon went to bed.

I fhould not have dwelled fo long on incidents
which may feem trifling, but as nothing more
material happened in the time, and my ftay in
this place [was] fomething longer than in any other
part of England (except Briftol), I thought better
to fill up the vacuum than to pafs over fo much
time entirely filent. I fhall now take my leave of
this town, which afforded me fuch an agreeable
variety, after I have given[2] fome defcription of it,
which I hitherto omitted. I differ with fome people
in opinion, who commonly begin with the geo-

---

[1] His failing.   [2] MS. has *give*.

graphical part, as I think the more time that can be given for forming a juft opinion of a fituation the beft method.

It ftands partly on the fide of a hill and is environed by many mountains; at a diftance, when you behold it from any of them, it makes a very agreeable appearance and feems as if en-clofed by the innumerable trees which furround it; it is watered by many rivulets and brooks, which flow very plentifully round, over which are many wooden bridges for the convenience of paffing. The town is compofed of half-a-dozen or feven large regular ftreets, well built, not in-cluding a number of fmaller lanes which run from many of them; and in the clofeft, and them which are moft expofed to dirt, they are kept fo decent that it gave me fome furprife. Near the town on one fide is a fountain or large refervoir[1] for water, which ftands on a high hill. This fupplies the town and is conveyed by a large pipe to the market crofs, whereon is a ciftern, and from thence is carried by fmaller pipes to every houfe. I do not remember anything elfe worth here inferting except what [has been] before related.

Having now done with Macclesfield, 'tis to be fuppofed we only waited for fome convenient opportunity of leaving it, and, upon inquiry,

---

[1] MS. has *reçevoir*.

[we] found a ftage-coach would fet out from Derby the Monday following, it being now Friday. It was, therefore, concluded to fet out for that place the next morning.

Our landlord provided us with horfes, and we fet out about ten, Saturday morning. He accompanied us to a compact town called Leek, where, having quitted us, we purfued our journey under the direction of a guide to Afhborne, a large town, where we found everything in great plenty. Here we refted this night.

The roads were almoft impaffable. Sometimes we were buried up to our horfes' bellies, and at others we rode on fuch dangerous precipices as had almoft endangered our falling. Certainly the roads in England are the moft difagreeable [part] of it, which they attribute to the fertility of the foil, and [that] is fo rich that the treading of a horfe roots up the ground.

As Derby is twelve miles from Afhborne, fo it was neceffary for us to be up early to overtake the ftage, and accordingly [we] fet out before day and got into Derby about ten o'clock. As my father rode, fo it prevented our making as much hafte as we otherwife fhould, was he not with us. But judge of our difappointment when we were informed of no ftage-coach going from thence till Wednefday !

This is a well-fituated and regular-built town. I can't forget that our entrance into it was odd enough, for I think we went under a bridge ; and as my ftay here was not above three hours, [I] cannot give a larger defcription of it.

The miffing the coach vexed us. Yet we were refolved not to be difappointed, for, having heard of another coach fetting off from Nottingham in the morning, we refolved to go thither, being about twelve miles from hence, and for that purpofe difmiffed our horfes and hired a coach to convey us to Nottingham. As the day proved extremely fine, it rendered our journey very agreeable.

We are now arrived at Nottingham, fo re-markable for the beauty and regularity of its buildings. Moft of the inhabitants here are Prefbyterians, and I really believe I was in five different meetings, which I miftook for churches, and at length was fo much vexed at being fo often difappointed, that I protefted againft look-ing further for one.

This town is compofed of a very large uniform fquare built on arches, which I call piazzas, as you can walk under moft of 'em ; feveral fine streets branch out from this square, and a number of 'em are planted with trees, cut and kept in excellent order. Its situation is extremely beautiful, as it is placed in the midst of a fine open country, and I have been assured the air in this town (though I am sure as big as Liverpool) is accounted as wholesome as any the country can afford, and certain it is the English have as just a taste for situation as perhaps any people in the world. As I am naturally curious, the time had insensibly slipped away, and was it not for the approach of night that minded me, I believe I should have stayed longer about the town. I returned to my lodging greatly pleased with what I had seen, when Valerius run up to me and said somewhat maliciously, " he hoped walking had filled my belly." I could not avoid smiling and told him " that I was glad to find he had employed his time better; that when we returned I could aver he had been in England, but hoped it would not be in my power to say he had only gone to be instructed how to make our Irish dishes as palatable as the English ;" for I afterwards understood he had been regaling himself over a quantity of dishes which were left at dinner, and which I found spread in great order.

When we had hired places and made some

little requifite preparations, we thought it ad-
vifable to go to bed, as the ftage fet off at two
in the morning. I had not got my firft fleep
when I was difturbed by a brawny maid, who
faid the coach was going. Valerius was fo much
vexed that he bid her to defire the coachman to
lay by his horfes for a couple of hours and he
would recompenfe him. As I had been informed
of the exactnefs of their proceedings, I could not
avoid laughing, which I did all the time of my
dreffing. After I had rallied him a little, he
conformed, and we were foon in a readinefs of
purfuing our journey.

We were fomething furprifed to find no other
places taken in the ftage than ours,[1] but withal
were well pleafed (though my father faid it would
be much eafier if it 'twas full, which by experience we found to be true). We had not gone
ten miles when we ftopped to take in a paffenger.
He was a man of few words, and therefore [I]
don't think 'tis any way pertinent to my ftory to
give him a particular defcription.

I very frequently regretted being fo confined
in thefe kind of vehicles, which afford no other
profpect than what you have infide, as there is
no glafs in 'em. Indeed, they correfponded with
Valerius his humour, for, if I don't forget, he

---

[1] MS. has *others*.

flept commonly very heartily. We went at a great rate, and very feldom altered our gait, except where a hill intervened, and then our coachman took the opportunity of giving his cattle breath.

As I had been faying fomething which I fuppofe difturbed Valerius, he ftarted up of a fudden, on which I congratulated him on receiving new life, as I termed it; he thanked me, and faid he only intended to propofe a topic and to fee who could manage it beft. I was glad he had reformed from fome of his old manners and was very impatient to be informed. He then began a differtation on how little fleep he had got, and on the vile cuftom of fetting off fo early, and added he, "let us not fpeak a word and lay a wager who can fleep longeft." As I knew his temper, I rallied him on the excellent choice he made of a fubject; after which he again fell into the arms of fleep.

I am extremely forry that nothing better offered to fupply the place of our trivial difcourfe (as I hinted before how clofe we were boxed); but then I cannot avoid paffing over fo long a journey in filence and fay I am arrived in London without fpeaking of fome of our company and how we paffed the time. Hitherto I have been fome-

thing ſevere on Valerius, who in reality is very
good-natured and readily partook of any of my
railleries, which he thought would conduce to
ſpending our time agreeably ; and indeed I ſhould
not have been ſo free with him was it not by his
own conſent, and he frequently takes a pleaſure
to hear of his behaviour in travelling, and though
ſleep was ſometimes his favourite topic, yet he
frequently hearkened to matters of greater conſe-
quence.

We now drew near to Leiceſter, when our
fellow-paſſenger ſaid we ſhould ſoon ſee the place
where King Richard the Third was buried.

" Ay, ay," cried Valerius, " I remember ſomething about it.   But ſhow me the place," added
he, " where he ſtood when he offered his kingdom for a horſe."

" Oh," replied our informer, laughing (in which
I accompanied him, as we remembered part of
the king's ſpeech in the play), " that was near
Boſworth, about ten miles acroſs the country,"
and to which he pointed.

" Right," anſwered Valerius; " I think Boſworth Field is painted on the ſcenes in the thea-
tre, where King Richard was killed by the Duke
of Richmond.   To be ſure I never played a part
in this tragedy, therefore I cannot give as juſt an

account of the plot as of many others by which
I have gained applaufe."

As we were thus diverting ourfelves, and admiring the ready recollection of Valerius, the
gentleman pointed over to a couple of fields,
where the ruins of an old building or monument
ftand, which he faid was erected to the memory
of King Richard, who was there interred.

This fight filled my mind with a kind of
horror on reflecting on the cruelty of that am-
bitious prince, which ferved to entertain me till
we arrived in the town of Leicefter. Breakfaft
was immediately fet, and certainly we ftood in
need of it, as we had travelled upwards of thirty
miles this morning without the leaft refreſh-
ment. I cannot avoid remembering one particular,
though very trifling. After we had very often
called for eggs, the waiter at length brought two
and protefted there was no more in town to be
bought. We were brought to think as he did,
for no more than fixpence was charged for eggs.

I rambled over as much of this town as the
time would permit. I take it to be as large as
Nottingham, though not comparable in the neatnefs of its buildings. Here is a very handfome
market-houfe, under which is an engine with
which they weigh the wagons. The contrivance

is admirable, for the horfes are not ftopped ; they only pull on the carriage, which when it is come on the proper place, the machine finks to the exact weight by fome large fprings, which are placed under it, and rifes even with the ground when the wagon is drawn off.

By a late Act of Parliament no wagon is to carry more than a certain weight, limited by faid act, to prevent the fpoiling of the roads, which in the winter are made exceeding deep by fuch great burdens as are frequently carried ; therefore this is a new contrivance to obferve that no rogueries are committed this way.

When I returned to the inn I found the coach ready harneffed, and [we] were informed we were to take in another paffenger, who foon appeared. His looks befpoke him agreeable. We foon re-affumed our places and proceeded on our way. After fome difcourfe with this new-comer I found he was an apothecary who refided in Lei-cefter, and that he was bound to London. He was a mighty well-tempered man, accompanied with fome humour, and gave us fome intelligence concerning the country. We had not gone above a mile when we ftopped at a very neat houfe and upon inquiry found we were to take in another paffenger, who foon appeared at the door, and

civilly aſked if any of us would drink wine, or
what moſt agreeable his houſe could afford. We
all replied in the negative except my father, who
aſked for a little ſmall drink.

As I ſhall ſoon have occaſion to ſpeak of this
gentleman, 'twill not be improper to give ſuch a
deſcription of him as I can draw from his appearance. The dreſs he wore made me take him to
be a clergyman, or elſe a Methodiſt preacher.
He ſeemed mightily reſerved, and betrayed ſomething ſevere or rigid in his countenance. I then
put all thoughts of mirth out of my head, as I
ſuſpected it would but ill ſuit with his temper;
however, I was willing to found him, and accordingly let ſomething fall concerning books. Here
'twas he took the blaze, and ſparkled in a manner
which ſurpriſed me. We talked but in general
for this day; neverthelefs, I found he was a
Preſbyterian miniſter who had laboured a great
deal on books, but to what intent I could not as
yet make any judgment. I could obſerve by
degrees the ſeverity of our clergyman ſomething
relaxed itſelf by a little familiarity, which made
our journey pleaſant, and in ſome manner com-
penſated for the proſpect of the country.

After three hours' ride the coach ſtopped at a
ſmall town called Market Harborough, remark-

able for nothing except a good inn, where we met with a very good dinner. We again embarked, and in about two hours and [a] half got into Northampton, a town, in my opinion, vieing with Nottingham, both for the regularity of its ftreets and its neatnefs. This has two fquares, whereas there is but one in Nottingham, and, in the opinion of feveral, is as large. As we got in early, I had leifure to view great part of it, in which the apothecary accompanied me, and civilly fhowed me all he knew. The great church and town-hall are juftly efteemed by all who fee them. We had juft as much time as was requifite for viewing them, and [I] fhall give fuch a defcription of' em as the fhortnefs of my ftay would permit.

The church is built of freeftone, carved with abundance of devices. It is in the form of a crofs, the tower ftanding in the middle. The part where divine fervice is celebrated is excef-fively well wrought, much in the fame tafte as[1] St. Thomas' Church in Liverpool. There are abundance of monuments of curious workman-fhip, and to examine it particularly would coft a man fome hours. This church was burned in a great fire which happened here in the reign of King Charles the Second. His Majefty allowed an hundred tons of timber, for the re-edifying it,

[1] MS. has *of.*

from fome of the adjoining mountains ; but the overfeers who delivered it being negligent, it is fuppofed as much more was taken, which did not complete the building. The contributions received towards it are[1] almoft incredible, amounting to more than twenty thoufand pounds fterling, a table of which is hung over the door.

The town-hall is built of much the fame ftone as the church, but as it is new, ftrikes the eye more agreeably. 'Tis a half fquare,* one [part] of which is for the king's ufe, and the other for the town. It is adapted for conveniency after the neweft tafte, no officer[s] having communication with each other. The king's court is adorned with fine paintings—of King William, Queen Mary, King George the Firft and Second, and Queen Caroline. It is very lofty, and much exceeds for convenience any court of judicature in Great Britain.

At our return we found fupper laid on the table. We foon attacked it with violence, and Valerius protefted we fhould not have [had] a bit for an hour, was it not for his diligence ; and after this laft fatigue was over, I hurried to bed. I fhall not fay I was difturbed from any dreams, but rather from a deadly fleep, which my early rifing, [and] the bruifes and jolts I received, occafioned. It was in vain to murmur when a man told me of

---

[1] MS. has *is*.

the ftage. I unwillingly obeyed this fummons, but
found all our company affembled in the parlour
regaling themfelves over fome hock and bread,
of which I tafted; and as Valerius is a very provi-
dent man, he propofed taking a bottle of white
wine in the coach, to wet his livers, as he faid.

We had not been long feated, when a fudden
gloom overfpread the fkies, and threatened an
immediate ftorm. This appeared difmal, as it
was not as yet daylight. We prepared ourfelves
by pulling up one of the windows, and foon
found it come on with unufual violence, accompanied with thunder and lightning. A melancholy filence reigned amongft us, and all but
Valerius were fecure from it, who, I can't fay by
what accident, got a horfe as we mounted the
ftage. It was impoffible for us to admit him, as
there was no perfon to mind the horfe, which, I
think, was to be left at the next town. I fhould
not have grudged him to fuffer for his impru-
dence, was I certain it would have been no other
damage to him than a little wetting, which we
afterwards were[1] glad to find was attended with
no worfe confequences.

The violence of the ftorm was not abated, when
we arrived at a fmall handfome town called New-

---

[1] MS. has *was.*

port Pagnell, where we got breakfaſt and Valerius
a dry ſhirt, who in reality wanted it ; and I muſt
confeſs I believe he ſuffered more from our gibes
than he did from the hurricane.

By the time we had done here, the clouds
diſſipated, and unveiled the ſun's cheerful rays,
and preſented us with a fine day. We again
mounted our vehicle, and in proportion as the
weather brightened our converſation enlivened,
and we became all mirth, ſave our clergyman,
who had no taſte for anything but books. He
ſpoke the French very well, and I muſt ſay I
think he was a man of parts, if he could have
diveſted himſelf of prejudice in ſome reſpects,
which was a great means of obſcuring them.

As I before obſerved, he ſpoke the French,
and as I could underſtand it tolerably, he ex-
plained ſome very remarkable paſſages in many
of the beſt French authors with judgment. From
hence we were inſenſibly led to talk of the merits of
ſome of our own, and [I] found he was very well
acquainted with the Engliſh ones. As I have ever
been a lover of my country, I thought in honour
I ought not paſs over in ſilence an eminent
genius who was of ſome ſervice to it, namely
Dean Swift, and accordingly aſked his opinion of
him. After he had knit his brows and put on a

more ferious air, he replied: " That he believed we
had more reafon to boaft of him than the French had
of Rabelais. He acknowledged he was excellent in
his own way, but that if he had taken as much
pains for the good of mankind he might have
made a great figure." Upon this I defired him to
explain himfelf and recount fome of his failings.

"I muft own," refumed he, "he had a little fpirit
of humour, but without judgment, and found[ed]
his characters according to his own peculiar way
of thinking. That really he was a general hater
of mankind ; reflected on the very fpecies for de-
ficiencies which were natural to the moft per-
fect, and from which no perfon is exempt ;"—
and [he] turned the vivacity and every bit of the
dean's humour into a bafenefs of mind, want of
judgment, and a fatirical reflection on mankind ;
—"that he lafhed at perfons in the moft eminent
ftations for the good they intended their country,
without examining to what end they purpofed
their defigns."

I muft confefs I was fomething furprifed at the
indigefted method he had of forming an opinion
of fo great a man's works, and was very forry
that this was his [Swift's] requital after forfeiting
fome of the greateft men's favour for his ingenuity
and the good of his country. Any one who has

read his works cannot but find an unbiaſſed diſ-
intereſtedneſs reign throughout, accompanied with
the moſt ſolid judgment, and though he hath ſomewhat a different turn of expreſſing himſelf (ſomething like ſatire), yet I take it to be the moſt
effectual method of giving the true meaning and
enforcing his arguments, which in ſome of his
ſubjects would loſe half the energy they ſo much
required, had they been wrote in any other ſtyle.

But to return. After I was recovered from
the ſurpriſe this unexpected harangue cauſed in
me, I was willing to ſay ſomething in defence of
my author, was it but barely for his being born
in the country. Nevertheleſs, I was unwilling to
urge my point too far, and for that purpoſe began
in the gentleſt manner poſſible. I ſaid that though
I muſt acknowledge Doctor Swift peculiar in his
way, yet I could not obſerve it paſſed further
than his private affairs ; that I fancied he had not
as yet made a proper diſtinction between him and
Monſieur Rabelais ; but without ſaying anything
further of Rabelais, as I think the ſubject of the
two authors no way connected. References from
one to the other are inſignificant. I added that he
could not be unacquainted with the great ſpirit of
party which reigned in his time, and the key
required to the reading his works, which, if a man

does not well underſtand, he frequently runs the
riſk of miſtaking his meaning. I ſaid I was
afraid he did not allow himſelf time to conſider
of theſe things before he gave his opinion, which
may in ſome meaſure be altered on recollection;
and told him I perceived he condemned him moſt
for railing at the diſcontent of party affairs, which
perhaps he thought neceſſarily incident to human
nature, which I knew ſubject to many changes,
but apprehended it did not go ſo far as to create
civil broils. As to any bits of humour which
you think beneath a man of his character, they
were only wrote at ſuch times as when he relaxed
himſelf from ſtudy, and to divert his friends,
which were all printed without his conſent—nay,
abſolutely againſt his command. He then aſked
me if I had any exception to make to what the
Earl of Orrery hath ſaid of him in a late treatiſe,
which was then juſt publiſhed. I anſwered I knew
little more than by what I heard, as I never read
more than a few pages of it, but, by what I could
infer, concluded that he dealt very ungenerouſly
by him, for he ſought the dean's acquaintance
with an unwearied zeal, and beſtowed on him vaſt
encomiums while alive, but ſince his death hath
wrote his criticiſms on him. Whether it redounds
much to a man's honour to attack the dead, when

he knows[1] he is not capable of defending himfelf, is a point every perfon may judge as he likes ;
" and," added I, " I always thought it incumbent
on a friend to endeavour to hide a man's foibles,
when he knows 'tis impoffible to reclaim 'em,
and [it] makes him in a manner acceffory to them,
when he was familiar with them, and did not ftrive
to amend them when there might[2] be a poffibility
of effecting it, the hopes of which is entirely loft
in death, which of confequence ought to cancel
any further remembrance of them."

He anfwered that he had afcribed all the merit
he deferved to him, and made him equal with fome
of the greateft geniufes, and endeavoured as a
friend to hide his foibles, which was contrary to
what I faid, but that they were fo glaring, 'twas
out of his power entirely to conceal them.

I replied, that it was the moft effectual method to make trivial faults have weight by recounting a man's excellencies, and, if I may fay
as an old fable, " Exalting him the higher to
make his fall the furer." It was by thefe means
Julius Cæfar loft his life, by hearkening to the
flattery of his creatures, who laid the blackeft
fcheme againft him, covering it and alluring him
with the bait of royalty, which they never in-

---

[1] MS. has *they know.*   [2] MS. has *may.*

tended to confer on him; and I am perſuaded
any man with Lord Orrery's talent need not be
afraid of getting applauſe without laying the
foundation of it on another's ruins; or, in the
words of inimitable Pope, who ſeemed to have
a juſt contempt of the baſeneſs of it—

> " Or if no baſis bear my riſing name,
> But the fallen ruins of another's fame :
> Then teach me, Heaven! to ſcorn the guilty bays,
> Drive from my breaſt that wretched luſt of praiſe,
> Unblemiſh'd let me live, or die unknown ;
> Oh, grant an honeſt fame or grant me none."

I concluded by ſaying, I hoped ſome perſon
would gain as much honour in vindicating Dean
Swift as my lord had by his criticiſms.

"Let us lay aſide the merit of his works,"
purſued he, "and come to his diſpoſition. Pray
is he not himſelf guilty of the greateſt breach of
friendſhip? When Mr. Pope wrote him ſeveral
fine letters in anſwer to ſome queſtions, he begged
and conjured him by all the ties they were under
not to make them public, which he afterwards
ungenerouſly printed, without even letting Mr.
Pope know."

I anſwered, that if he barely conſidered the
fact without circumſtances, he was; but then the
Dean was a man of ſo good principles, that he

knew he could never be accountable to the world, if he deprived it of fuch valuable effects as any of Pope's productions.

Whether it was out of a point of manners, or that he found fome juftice in what I urged, I can't fay, but he here defifted, and faid, in fpite of argument, every man would retain his own opinion; upon which Valerius ftarted up and faid that his opinion was, and he would retain it, that eating a good piece of beef was the beft argument. For his part, he did not care if neither of our authors were ever born, and that he did not underftand peoples' contefting about men they never faw.

Though he had not all the reafon in the world to back this opinion, yet it ferved to difcontinue farther arguments on this head, which made me forget to mention two fmall towns we paffed through while it lafted, viz. Oborn [Woburn] and Hockley-in-the-Hole, remarkable for nothing but their neatnefs.

Not far from the laft of thefe towns our coach made a full ftop. The frequent robberies committed on thefe roads made us fufpect we were going to be attacked by fome of 'em. We were foon undeceived when our driver told us he wanted to fhow us a remarkable tree, which no-

body could tell what it was, or how long it hath
been there. I viewed it from the coach-door.
It feemed to be very old, overgrown with a kind
of mofs, but not fo clofe ; the branches extended
a good length, and its leaves looked fomething
like fham-rocks.[1] For curiofity I took a few
fprigs of it, and had them till they quite decayed.

About an hour afterwards we got to a town
called Dunftable, where we made a very hearty
dinner, when our clergyman told us he was
obliged to quit us, as he intended going to fee a
friend four miles off. Though we had fpoke of
fome points that neither of us would agree in,
yet I could have wifhed for his company to
London. I went over this place, and found
nothing worth remarking except fome odd infcriptions over the market-houfe.

We feated ourfelves, and purfued our journey
full of fpirits ; and having paffed through fome
infignificant villages, arrived in the town of St.
Albans, a place fo noted in Englifh hiftory. I
had juft time to get the fexton of the church to
view the curiofities I had heard fo often of.

We entered a door which conducted us to a
very long antique aifle, where feveral monuments

[1] MS. has *fham-rogues*, which may be *phonetically* correct.

ftand, and appear very folemn by a feeble light
that is conveyed by many old windows. It
branches out into many leffer walks, in which
are a number of old garlands hung over the
burying-places of young people, and is inter-
fperfed with ftatues or reliques of faints. At one
fide is a long entry or paffage, wherein are a
number of fmall doors, which, they fay, formerly
led to as many cells, where confeffion was heard,
and adjoining ftood a monaftery, but now quite
down, except part of the foundation, which may
be perceived. We again returned into the large
aifle, in the middle of which the fexton clapped
his hands, when I believe it was echoed by five
hundred claps, which gradually died away, and
feemed to lofe the found at both the extremities.
Some people have attempted to account for it.
Some of their reafons we were told, but as none of
them feem to carry any weight of probability, [I]
fhall not here mention any of them. From hence
we paffed into the part where divine fervice is
performed, which makes an odd appearance like
the reft. Here we faw a quantity of reliques of
abbots. I noticed a couple—the fkull of a man
which had lain there upwards of three hundred
years, wherein the teeth were as white and as faft
as could be ; likewife the thigh-bone of a man of

an immoderate fize. From hence we doubled
round a couple of obfcure aifles leading to the
parifh veftry-room, in the midft whereof ftand
the ftumps of fix old pillars. Thefe, it is faid,
are the remains of a fhrine or tomb, wherein an
abbot was enfhrined for feveral hundred of years
paft, and lay among the ruins of the church,
when moft part of it and the monaftery was
rafed in the civil wars, and [they] happened to
find them when the rubbifh was removed to
make a veftry-room.

We went to the outfide of the large aifle,
where I faw a large iron monument erected to
the memory of the good Duke Humphrey, who
was not only a learned man, but a good patriot.
He was Lord Protector of England during the
minority of King Henry the Sixth, who awhile
after his acceffion to the throne efpoufed Mar-
garet, the daughter of René,[1] Duke of Anjou
and Lorraine, who foon formed her a party that
ruled, giving the king little more than a fhadow
of authority fave the title ; who was a temperate
and mild prince, and fought, perhaps, more to
pleafe his confort than to look into the concerns
of his fubjects. As Duke Humphrey, who, by

[1] MS. has *Renate*, a free tranflation of the Latin form
Renatus.

his prudence, and alfo by the honour and authority which his birth and place gave, did not feem
willing to let the queen and her creatures govern
in fome refpeds which he thought prejudicial
to his country, oppofed her and her party, they
fearing the like in feveral matters they were
willing to introduce, refolved to be rid of fo
great an obftacle. Many great lords were fe-
duced into this confpiracy ; at this time the Parliament was held at St. Edmundfbury, where,
when this great duke came to appear, [he] was
arrefted under pretence of high treafon by Lord
Beaumont, then high conftable, and the Dukes of
Buckingham, Somerfet, and others of the conju-
ration. He was not long in prifon, when he
was found dead, and his body afterwards fhown
to the Lords and Commons, as if he had died of
an impofthume or palfy. As he was accufed for
contriving the king's deftrudion, thereby to get the
crown, his friends feared they might[1] ufe his body
ignominioufly, and for that purpofe conveyed it
privately to St. Albans (where I am now), and
buried him, and it was kept fo clofe a fecret that
it never was found out where he was laid, till
about forty years ago. When fome labourers were
digging to make a vault, they accidentally met

[1] MS. has *may.*

with ſome ſteps, which they purſued till they got
to a ſmall arch, and, entering in there, found an
old oak coffin, which having broke, [they] met
with a lead one, and, opening it, [they] were ſurpriſed to find [it] full of a liquor, and a body
lying in it without the leaſt putrefaction, it being
as firm and hard, and the hair as freſh, as that
of a living perſon; it retained the very colour,
though it could not be interred leſs than three
hundred years. There are ſeveral old inſcriptions
round this place, which intimate his coming there.
Everybody at finding him was curious to ſee
him, and very unwiſely they let people dip their
fingers in the liquor to endeavour to find what it
was made of; as likewiſe phyſicians took phials
of it for the ſame intent, and by theſe means
conſumed it, after which his fleſh dropped to
powder, but the bones as yet remain there, which
I took ſingly in my hands. He ſeemed to be a
man of low ſtature,[1] but exceeding ſtrong. The
apothecary dipped his finger in the bottom of
the coffin, and told me there was ſomething of a
fluid, which I found likewiſe.

In all probability I ſhould have ſtayed here
longer, had not a meſſenger come and told us the
coach waited, and accordingly [we] haſtened to

¹ MS. has *nature.*

the inn, where our company expected us. I was
very well pleafed, as I had feen all without the
leaft lofs of time, and indeed more would have
been ufelefs.

Having again taken our places, we foon
arrived in a fmall town called Barnet, and in a
fhort fpace got on a large open plain called
Finchley Common, fo celebrated for the frequent
robberies and murders committed there; and our
apothecary, to animate us, told us of his knowing
five ftage-coaches to be robbed by a fingle man,
and they altogether; and certain it is a day
feldom paffes without fomething of this kind
being here practifed. We travelled here under
fome anxiety, and fufpected every bufh for a tory.
Many gibbets are up over all this common, and
I faw no lefs than five within a piftol-fhot of each
other, which made [me] wonder it did not deter
thefe villains from fuch practices.

This common is fix or feven miles long, and
we were not a little pleafed when we had paffed
it over without the leaft moleftation, and got to
Highgate, which I believe is part of the fuburbs
of the city of London, as it is almoft a continued
ftreet to it. Here it is that they are fworn to
feveral comical oaths, with a pair of horns on 'em,
of which there are a great number here on poles

M

outfide the doors, and you are made free at a fmall expenfe. This place is fituated on an eminence, which affords you the profpect of the vaft city of London. Tho' mightily obfcured by the clouds of fmoke which arife from it, I viewed [it] on all fides, but could find no end to this metropolis, which is adorned with fo many lofty fpires and public buildings that imagination cannot paint a more beautiful profpect at a diftance. We rolled down this gentle defcent, and foon found ourfelves on the rugged pavement of the city, which is prodigioufly uneafy to thofe who pafs in wheel-carriages; and, after many fevere jolts, we ftopped at the Ram in Smithfield, where the ftage puts up. This is a difagreeable inn, but as it was now too late to feek for a further and more convenient lodging, and being much fatigued, [we] thought it better to get to bed. We travelled in thefe two laft days upwards of one hundred and twenty-fix miles. I never faw Valerius fo much dejected, and could not even draw the leaft piece of humour from him.

The next morning I found myfelf very much refrefhed, and concluded the firft bufinefs fhould be to find out a more convenient abode. I remembered to have got a direction where the Irifh commonly fet up; and, having procured a guide, [I] defired him to fhow me to the Three Cups in

Bread Street, where my father was to follow me in a coach, in which I would not accompany him, as I chofe rather to fee the town.

I can't fay whether I appeared like Roderick Random at his firft coming to London; but for my life I could not avoid remembering his comrade Strap, as often as I looked on Valerius, who looked with his mouth half open at the great variety in the ftreets. I think I prevented his falling twice, as he very feldom looked down to mind his way, and he had more than once ftumbled againft the pofts which are fet up for footpaffengers ; withal faying he believed the people here were fools to put fuch nuifances in their ftreets.

After we had fixed our lodging (at the place mentioned) we again fallied out and viewed many ftreets till 'Change time, where I was obliged to go to find perfons to whom I had letters. I was furprifed to find fuch a concourfe of people as refort here from all nations, and the noble branch of commerce as it is carried on here fo regular amidft nothing but confufion : every creature feemed intent on his proper bufinefs. I found out my countrymen, amongft whom I knew a few. As I was very often at this place, I had an opportunity of taking particular notice on't, and for that purpofe took fome notes.

This ftately piece is fituated in Cornhill, almoft
in the middle of the ftreet, and is a fquare, though
fomething longer than broad; or, to term it better,
it is an oblong. On every fide is a noble piazza,
fupported by many columns and arches, on which
the galleries ftand. The outfide of the building
is of much larger dimenfions, and to the front of
Cornhill is another row of pillars, or a piazza, in
the middle of which ftands a large gate, as likewife another to the oppofite fide. Over the firft
gate mentioned is a handfome fteeple (if it may
be called fo) of a great height, with chimes in it.
Under the piazza are large cellars, over which
are fhops that let for a great rent. 'Tis all built
of white carved ftone, and greatly enriched with
the feveral orders of architecture, which as I don't
thoroughly underftand, [I] fhall not come to
particulars. At each fide in the middle are feveral
arms, as follow :—On the north fide the king's,
on the fouth thofe of the city, on the eaft Sir
Thomas Grefham's, who founded it, and on the
weft the arms of the Company of Mercers. There
are a great number of niches filled with ftatues of
the kings and queens of England, with divers
infcriptions which I could not well read. Withinfide all around are many niches, but moft of them
vacant. The piazza is paved with black and
white marble, and [you] defcend by one ftep into

the vaſt area, in the middle whereof ſtands a noble
ſtatue of King Charles the Second on a lofty
pedeſtal, which is adorned with ſeveral devices,
and under are[1] written theſe words :—

CAROLO CÆSARI BRITANNICO.

*Patriæ Patri, Regum Optimo, Clementiſſimo,
Auguſtiſſimo, Generis Humani Deliciis, Utriuſq.
Fortunæ Victori, Pacis Europæ Arbitro, Maris
Domino & Vindici.*

*Societas Mercatorum Adventuror. Angliæ (quæ
per* CCCC. *jam propè annos regiâ benignitate
floret) Fidei Intemeratæ, Gratitudinis æternæ Teſti-
monium, venerabunda poſuit.*[2]

On the weſt ſide of the pedeſtal is a Cupid
with a ſhield, wherein are the arms of England
and France, another on the north with the arms
of Ireland, and on the eaſt thoſe of Scotland.
This place is ſo well divided into walks, that you
may eaſily find a man of any country in the world.
When I had finiſhed here, I went to an eating-
houſe and dined, where having met a friend, he
propoſed after dinner ſhowing me Guild-Hall, as
it lay contiguous to us. I accepted the offer,[3] and
in leſs than half an hour walked to it.

---

[1] MS. has *is*.
[2] Collated with Stow, ed. 1720, book 2, p. 137.
[3] MS. has *it*.

This ftructure lies at one end of King Street, and is the town-houfe of this large city. There is a kind of portico, through which we paffed to the principal hall. 'Tis very large, but feems to be old. On the right hand, at the upper end, is the Court of Huftings, and at the other end, oppofite to it, are the Sheriffs' Courts. There are alfo againft fome pillars the arms of St. Edward the Confeffor and of the kings of England, the fhield and crofs of St. George, as alfo the arms of London and of the twelve companies. The portraitures of King William and Queen Mary are here drawn in full length, with feveral judges on either fide who were of fome fervice to the city. From this hall we went up fome ftairs to the Mayor's Court; though not magnificent, yet [it] anfwers the end for electing of fheriffs and other officers, and [it is] where they entertain ambaffadors and other great men on certain days.

From hence we took a long round, and my guide told me I was near Leaden-Hall Market (by all accounts I had heard the fineft in Europe). This market is divided into large fquares, each fquare or place appointed only to fell one thing. All manner of eatables are here fold, and it looks like a town moftly compofed of fhops. The walks all around are covered, fo that you are

fecured in the wetteft weather. They fell baize
and other manufactures here on certain days.

Night was juft approaching by the time I had
taken a view of this unparalleled market, though
a man without money in his pocket may as com-
pletely ftarve in it as if he was in the moft un-
known place on the continent of Africa or
America.

At my return I found Valerius preparing to
go to bed, and as foon as it was dufk I did the
like, intending to be up early with an intention
to view St. Paul's, etc. ; but there were[1] fo many
charms on the pillow that I could not force myfelf to rife till eight o'clock. Having procured
a guide, Valerius and I fet out, and my father
followed, for our impatience would not permit
us to wait for him.

After a fmall walk we arrived in the yard
belonging to the Church, which is a large piece
of ground, well built, in the midft whereof
ftands this furprizing ftructure, which, as it is
fituated on an eminence, it adds the more to its
height; and though the Cathedral of St. Peter's
in Rome is faid to exceed it in the richnefs of its
materials, yet travellers affirm St. Paul's makes a
much grander appearance, as that of St. Peter's
is much obfcured (except at on[e] front) by the

[1] MS. has *was.*

Palace of the Vatican and many other buildings contiguous to it, whereas St. Paul's may be viewed all round. The circuit outfide the walls of this Church is 2292 feet. The dome or cupola is placed in the midft of the fabrick, and at the weft end are two high towers, making the front of the edifice. The outfide is adorned with innumerable pilafters of the different orders, and [the fpaces] between the arches of the windows are enriched with feftoons, cherubim, fruit, leaves, Bifhops' caps, books, and the Dean's arms, with many other devices I cannot recollect, all elegantly cut in ftone. At the weft end are[1] acroteria of the figures of the Twelve Apoftles, with that of St. Paul on the angle, with thofe of the four Evangelifts furrounded by angels, and over the dials of the clock are[2] the two towers: thefe are adorned with many pilafters, and at the top of each is a curious pine-apple. The infide of the Church is fupported by lofty pillars, wrought after the moft elegant tafte ; the cupola is fupported by eight of them, and to look to the top or vertex, would almoft ftrain the eyes, being 276 feet high, in which are painted the Twelve Apoftles ; they appear, as you think 'em, very diminutive, but in reality are incredibly large. The pillars which fupport the roof of the church are in

[1] MS. has *is an*.   [2] MS. has *on*.

two ranges, with beautiful arches, which divide
the body of the church from the choir, and make [1]
three [a]isles; the floor [is] paved throughout
with marble, except under the cupola, which is
laid with fine polished porphyry ; the altar piece
is adorned with fluted pillars, the capitals of them
gilt, over which is a glory finely painted; the north
and south entrance are by iron doors, exceeding
by far any work of the kind in Great Britain,
executed by the famous Monsieur Tijan; the
galleries, Bishop's throne, Lord Mayor's seat and
stalls, add to the beauty of it, forming altogether
a curious piece of wainscot most curiously carved.

We ascended to the outside of the dome by
a great number of large winding steps, where is
a stone gallery surrounding the base of the cupola.
We then entered the inside of it, which looks
into the church, and is fenced by a neat iron rail.
This is called the whispering gallery, and it really
surprized me to find the softest whisper resounded
by an infinite number. I viewed several people
walking in the aisle, who appeared to me as the
Liliputians did to Gulliver when he first saw
'em. I walked several times round this place,
and was conducted between the two roofs to
some wooden stairs, which led to the very top of

---

[1] MS. has *and divide* . . . *which make.*

the cupola. After I [had] mounted many flights we
entered the upper gallery, fenced with an iron
banifter, almoft as high again as the whifpering
gallery. The pedeftal rifes from hence, which
fupports the ball and crofs (the crofs being ten
foot high). I walked feveral times about this,
but indeed I thought I fhould be blown off. I
faw feveral coaches paffing under me, which feemed
like fo many children's toys ; the numberlefs
fteeples in the City of London appeared like fo
many mafts of fhips, and the entire town and
country looked like an agreeable landfkip, which
we fometimes admire after the hand of an eminent
artift ; the houfes here, being covered with red
tiles, made the objeét more ftriking, and I ftayed
upwards of an hour to behold this real fcene,
which looked fo imaginary.

This undefcribable piece of building ftands on
the ruins of the old church, which was burned
by lightning, when *King James* gave a commiffion for colleéting fubfcriptions for the rebuilding
it ; but the fire happened[1] foon after, which demolifhed it fo much that it was neceffary to pull
it entirely down, whereupon *King Charles* the
Second commiffioned[2] for rebuilding it agreeable
to a model drawn up by Sir Chriftopher Wren,
furveyor of the works. His Majefty allowed

---

[1] MS. has *happening*.   [2] Gave a commiffion.

£1000 towards it, and the private fubfcriptions amounted to upwards of feventy thoufand pounds, which fum being too fmall for fo great an under-taking, an Act of Parliament paffed for a duty of two fhillings per chaldron on all coals brought into the Port of London from the 1ft of May till Midfummer, and from thence to Michaelmas three fhillings per chaldron, one fourth of which was allowed to this building, and the reft to public ufes. By an other Act of[1] James the Second a duty on coal at eighteenpence the chaldron [was impofed] for three years [for this purpofe], except the one-fifth, which was applied to public ufe. By an Act of[2] William the Third a duty of one fhilling per chaldron [was impofed] for eight years [for this purpofe], except the one-fixth for public ufe. By an Act of[3] Anne a duty of two fhillings per chaldron [was impofed] for eight years for compleating and adorning St. Pauls, and to purchafe fome old houfes which ftood in the way, and to fecure it from fire. All which benevolence and benefactions amounted to between feven and eight hundred thoufand pounds, which have been employed in building and fecuring this magnificent fabrick.

When I had fufficiently viewed the town, I defcended by the wooden ftairs, and, when I came to the ftone gallery, was furprized to find Valerius

---

[1] MS. has *in.*   [2] MS. has *in.*   [3] MS. has *in.*

bufy at carving his name on a fpout, which for certain would prove to any of his countrymen who fhould come after him that he was there, and fo [he] purfued his work, withal defiring and preffing me to follow his example. I yielded at laft to his entreaties, but not to his fatisfaction, for I only cut the two firft letters of my name flightly, whereas his was in full length and deeply cut. I did not entirely let him put the finifhing ftroke to it, but we hafted down, as we had left my father waiting almoft two hours ; where when we met with him, we went to the Exchange, but entertaining ourfelves by the way with the grandeur of St. Pauls.

After we had finifhed our parade, we adjourned to the eating-houfe I had been before at. After dinner I told Valerius we would go to a houfe where I was afraid he would be kept. He was very impatient to know it; when I told him it was Bedlam, he faid he would take care how he would behave, and having procured a guide we foon got to the mad-houfe.

The Hofpital of Bethlehem, commonly called Bedlam, is a fair large ftructure, built of brick, except the principal corners and tracings, which are Portland ftone. It ftands in Moorfields, in an open place, in good air; it is furrounded by handfome gravel walks and trees, kept in order. We entered into a long aifle or paffage, divided

by an iron door, feparating the men from the
women. In this entry are abundance of fmall
doors leading to as many cells, where the lunatics
are kept. Thefe poor creatures are kept under
fuch difcipline that they tremble when they fee
any of the officers belonging to the houfe. We
were not long there, when a man accofted us with
a book in his hand, without any covering on his
head. He told us he was a clergyman, who, in
compaffion to the poor creatures here confined,
came often to read to them, and that as he was
acquainted with[1] the houfe, [he] would fhew it to
us. He fpoke this fo ferioufly, that if I was not
previoufly acquainted with his diforder, [I] fhould
not have fufpected him for madnefs. Accordingly he went over moft of the houfe, and called
to feveral in their cells ; and fays he, " I'll fhew
you a fon of a b——h of an Irifhman, who is here
for cutting off his mother's head ;" when we found
him in fact to be an Irifhman. We peeped in
the hole for that purpofe, and faw him picking
ftraws, with a landfkip of chalk before him.
The poor man who conducted us had been in
here for ten years, and was a man of learning.
He was now recovering, and was permitted to
walk the gallery. It would be endlefs to recount
the many deplorable circumftances thefe unhappy

[1] MS. has *in.*

people are under here ; I proteft I infenfibly grew
melancholy, and hafted away not to be longer a
fpectator of their calamities, which put in my mind
God's goodnefs for not inflicting fuch punifhments
on[1] many finners whofe crimes are very notorious.

After we had walked round a great part of this
place, we returned to our lodgings, where we
met my father, who faid he intended to go to
Vauxhall. This elated Valerius ; and for that purpofe [we] went to Queenhithe Stairs, and found
a number of boatmen, who I thought were making
a jeft of me ; for they have a method of holding
up one of their fingers, crying aloud, " Sculls or
oars." The difference of 'em is, the fculls have
but one man, but the oars have two. When I
found my miftake, I got into one of their boats,
and arrived at Vauxhall at feven o'clock. The
garden ftrikes the eye prodigioufly, as it is fet
with many rows of tall trees, kept in excellent
order, among which are placed an incredible
number of globe lamps, by which it is illuminated ; and when they are lighted, the[2] found
of the mufic ravifhing the ear, added to
the great refort of company fo well dreffed,
and walking all about, would almoft make one

---

[1] MS. has *of*.

[2] MS. has *and the found*, and in the next line, *which*, *if
added*—which makes a grammatical chaos.

believe he was in the Elysian Fields: some [were]
reposing themselves on banks, others reading,
and some conversing, which forms so delightful a
variety, that the soul is insensibly transported out
of its common sphere. This is a general place of
rendezvous, where intrigues of all sorts are commonly carried on, and pity it is that so enchanting a place is so often made the instrument of so
much wickedness. Many women in some sort
owe their ruin to it, for, when their spirits are so
much elevated by all these charms, they seldom
are capable of reflection, and do not consider of
the harm till it is too late. However, I think it
should be preferred to the masquerade, where
people mask, and frequently practise many im-
modest matters, which they can the better do as
not being known,[1] and [it] is a much greater trap
for young maidens than any yet invented:

> " What guards the purity of melting maids
> At courtly balls and midnight masquerades ?"—POPE.

As I do not pretend to set up for a reformer of
the times, I shall not dwell farther on this sub-
ject, but observe that I should not choose (was I
to marry) a woman who had much used those
kind of amusements.

In the middle of the garden are two femi-

[1] MS. has *been.*

circles which appear like an amphitheatre, in
which are placed a great number of fmall booths,
which may contain about fix or eight people
a-piece, where they commonly refrefh themfelves
with fweetmeats, wine, tea, coffee, or fuch like.
The backs of thefe boxes, or booths, are adorned
with curious paintings, all which are enlightened
to the front with globes. They are all numbered,
and very juft attendance is given by a vaft number
of waiters kept for that purpofe. Near to this is
a grand orcheftra, where the mufic plays in fine
weather; but this night the concert was held in
a magnificent hall neatly furnifhed. At one fide
of the orcheftra is a noble ftatue of Handel.
The mufic no fooner began than we entered the
hall, where fifty-four muficians performed. Mr.
Lowe foon fang, whofe charaƈter I need not here
mention, and after him the inimitable Mifs Burchell, whofe voice I believe exceeds all in Europe.
She but lately hath come into repute, and was
accidentally found out by a gentleman who happened to be at a houfe in the north of England
(where fhe ferved in quality of a chambermaid);
and having heard her hum a fong, and being
furprized at her voice, at his return to London [he]
reported it to the proprietor of Vauxhall, who
fent for her, and had her inftruƈted by the beft

mafters; and [fhe] is now arrived to fuch[1] perfection as aftonifhes almoft every one that hears her.
When fhe was done, the formerly celebrated Mifs
Stephens performed, before accounted the beft
finger in Great Britain, but indeed her voice[2]
feemed very infipid after that of Mifs Burchell.

As we returned to the booths, my father by
chance efpied a gentleman with whom he was
acquainted. He had been here fome time to ftudy
the law, and I had the pleafure of reading in the
news foon after I came home of his being admitted a barrifter-at-law. He introduced us to
an old Frenchwoman and an agreeable girl, her
daughter, who received us in an affable manner.
I underftood afterwards that he lodged at her
houfe in Chelfea, "where," added he, "I fhall
be glad to have your company, and from thence
we will proceed to Ranelagh." The old lady and
her daughter preffed us fo much that we promifed to be punctual. I foon grew very great
with the old dame, who was very entertaining,
and very freely called me her child. I could not
tell what conftruction to put on this adventure,
but in the mean [time] was well pleafed at having
met my friend.

Whilft we were thus entertaining ourfelves, we

---

[1] MS. has *the*.   [2] MS. has *it*.

were informed of the new cafcade being lighted.
The old woman leaned on my fhoulder to prevent
her falling, and, gabbling French, got to the
cafcade in this pofture. A fine grotto faluted our
eyes, furrounded by the ftatues of Neptune, a
mermaid, and other fea-pieces, as dolphins, &c.,
fome reclining on the banks, and placed in very
agreeable attitudes, behind which fell in cafcades
cryftal water, which[1] was received by a fpacious
bafin or refervoir,[2] wherein were[3] placed fmall
fifhes, &c., which fpouted up the water. It was
all painted in water-colours, and fo well executed
that it hath often deceived many for real water.
The lights were placed at the infide with fuch
exactnefs that [they] reprefented everything very
natural[ly], and an innumerable quantity of 'em
are behind, though not vifible.

While we were admiring this piece of art, Mifs
Burchell (we were told) was going to give a
favourite fong. As I am a lover of mufic, I
bounced away, not remembering the lady in my
care, who called after me, and faid fhe was afraid
fhe would be trod by the crowd ; but my impatience hurried me fafter than fhe could well go ;
and whether it was chance or otherwife I can't
fay, but fhe fell down, faying fhe had broke her

---

[1] MS. has *and*.   [2] MS. has *receivoir*.   [3] MS. has *was*.

arm. This accident difpleafed me, and fome people may be fo ill-natured as to fay 'twas rather the fear of lofing the fong than the fear of her arm that vexed me. I raifed her as foon as poffible, and in a manner dragged her to the hall, where Mifs had juft begun[1] her fong. My dame puffed fo immoderately that it partly interrupted my hearing. When Mifs had gotten the juft applaufe of her performance, we returned to our booth, when my partner offered to fet me down in her coach near my lodgings; but, as Valerius waited, [I] was obliged to decline this obliging offer. When they departed, I found him out, and having got a boat, though it began to blow, we fafely landed at Queenhithe Stairs, and foon got to our lodgings.

Though the next morning proved wet, yet we had fome bufinefs which obliged us to go to Spitalfields,[2] and for that purpofe got a coach, where in lefs than an hour we were fet down. There is a large fquare in this place, and many good ftreets. A great number of French re-fugees have fettled here, and they reckon no lefs than ten thoufand French or their defcendants now in this parifh, moft of 'em following the filk bufinefs, and [thefe] may be efteemed the largeft

[1] MS. has *began*.   [2] MS. has *Spittle Fields*.

filk manufactures in Europe, little elfe being here
wove. The parifh books here mention two
thoufand houfes in thefe[1] fields, and upwards of
eighteen thoufand fouls.

Moft of the day being fpent here, we returned
to our lodging to drefs for Ranelagh, and in an
hour after we got a coach, and directed him to
drive to Chelfea; and having paffed through
many agreeable roads (moft of which are hung
with lamps) leading to Ranelagh, we got to
this lovely village, wherein are many handfome
houfes, many of which are let out to the nobility
in the fummer feafon, as the air here is accounted
the beft near London. We immediately got the
houfe by the direction our friend had given us,
who received us with all the marks of civility.
We were conducted to an upper room command-
ing a profpect of the city; but how great was
my furprife when I found the old lady and her
daughter undreffed, and of confequence unpre-
pared for Ranelagh. They made fome excufe
for not accompanying us, and immediately the
tea-table was fet, with fome fine buns which the
village is remarkable for. It is a particular man
who makes them, and [he] is faid to difpofe of
more than two thoufand every Sunday. They

[1] MS. has *thofe*.

have fomewhat a different flavour from any I ever
before ate. When Queen Caroline was living, happening one day to take the air this way, and having
heard fo much of this man's buns, fhe bought
[fome] of them, and the owner of the houfe,
who ferved her, requefted the liberty of putting
up her majefty's arms, and calling it hers, which
fhe granted, and accordingly the arms are up,
and [it] retains the title of the Royal Bun Houfe
ever fince.

Tea being over, we took our places in the
coach, and about five or fix minutes after we
were fet down at the door leading to the gardens,
which, though but fmall, yet are laid out in a
very judicious manner, and therein[1] are feveral
fifh-ponds or canals, but whether there are any
fifh in them or no [I] fhall not refolve. The place[2]
ftands near the river Thames, but is deprived from
a communication to it by fome fields overgrown
with twigs, &c., which lie between it and the river,
[and] which the proprietor was unfairly deprived
of. The manner was thus : This piece of ground
was advertized to be let, when this man applied to
the landlord to take it, thereby to render the
gardens more commodious, and accordingly
agreed for a certain fum ; but the proprietor of

---

[1] MS. has *wherein.*   [2] MS. has *It.*

Vauxhall, hearing of it, and knowing that if fo much ground was added to Ranelagh, thereby[1] adding to it the profpect of the river and the oppofite houfes, it might prevent people from[2] going to his gardens, immediately went[3] to the landlord and agreed to give him double the price the other man was to have it for, whereupon he got it. The proprietor of Ranelagh could lay no claim according to law, as there had been no writings between him and the owner of the land, which the proprietor of Vauxhall now lets to be entirely overrun with rufhes and ufelefs ftuff, whereby the profpect of the river is entirely loft.

When I had taken a walk all round the gardens, I went into the Amphitheatre, which is very large, entirely built of timber ; all around are booths placed, fuch as before-mentioned at Vauxhall, though a greater quantity of them, and [you] defcend by one ftep into the area, where feveral tea tables are laid out ; over the booths rife very ftately windows, outfide of which is a gallery encompaffing the whole. From the crown of the arches of the windows a cap or cupola decreafes[4] gradually, till it terminates in a point above, out of which the chimney of the

---

[1] MS. has *and thereby*.   [2] MS. has *may* . . . . *of*.
[3] MS. has *goes*.   [4] MS. has *decreafed*.

great fire-place below is conveyed. This fire-place ſtands in the middle, from whence all the tea-tables are ſupplied with water and coffee. The room is illuminated with thirty-ſix branches of globe lamps, beſides many others, which are put near the booths. The orcheſtra fronts the door, wherein was an excellent band of muſic and a good organ. The ſingers here are not ſo good as at Vauxhall. Mrs. Storer ſung Ellina Roon in Iriſh, but with ſuch a clipping of the words that I was aſſured by one who well underſtood Iriſh that was ſhe to ſing it in Ireland it would be taken for ſome other dialect. Mr. Beard performed next, but the tune was ſo melancholy, no body paid it much attention. Here was a moſt brilliant appearance; and moſt of the Court come here. The maſquerade is commonly kept at this place.

The many repeaters which ſtruck here minded me that the hours ſlid away more haſtily than I choſe, and at eleven o'clock we retired. Having called for our coach, we and our friend placed ourſelves, but the incredible quantity of coaches that occupied both ſides of the paſſage detained us near an half an hour, and I really believe the lane we went through was near a mile. Our friend. parted [from] us before we got free, and

it was near one o'clock before we were fet down
at our lodgings.

Next day Valerius and I fet out to take a view
of the Monument (having hitherto only feen it
at a diftance), and in a fhort fpace arrived at this
noble column, being fluted to the iron gallery,
and [it] ftands on a grand pedeftal ; it is upwards
of 200 feet high, built of Portland ftone. On the
top, over the iron gallery, is a pedeftal, on which
ftands a gilded flame. The weft fide of the
lower pedeftal contains a reprefentation of the
dreadful Fire of London in the year 1666, which
happened in a baker's houfe. This is fo well
known that I need not here fpeak particularly
of it. The infcriptions on each fide of the pillar
give a fmall defcription of it ; they are wrote in
Latin, which I tranfcribed, but choofe to infert
'em here in Englifh, as I met 'em fomewhere
tranflated by an eminent hand.

ON THE NORTH SIDE.

" In the year of Chrift 1666, the 2nd day of
September, eaft from hence, at the diftance of
202 feet (the height of this column), about midnight, a moft terrible fire broke out, which, driven
on by a high wind, not only wafted the adjacent
parts, but alfo places very remote, with incredible

noise and fury. It confumed 89 churches, the city gates, Guildhall, many public ftructures, hofpitals, fchools, libraries, a vaft number of ftately edifices, 13,200 dwelling-houfes, 400 ftreets. Of twenty-fix wards, it utterly deftroyed fifteen, and left eight others fhattered and half burnt. The ruins of the City were 436 acres, from the Tower by the Thames fide to the Temple Church, and from the north-eaft gate along the City Wall to Holborn Bridge. To the eftates and fortunes of the citizens it was mercilefs, but to their lives very favourable, that it might in all things refemble the laft conflagration of the world.

" The deftruction was fudden, for in a fmall fpace of time the fame city was feen moft flourifhing, and reduced to nothing.

" Three days after, when this fatal fire had baffled all human counfels and endeavours, in the opinion of all, as it were by the Will of Heaven, it ftopt, and on every fide was extinguifhed "

ON THE SOUTH SIDE.

" Charles the Second, fon of Charles the Martyr, King of Great Britain and Ireland, Defender of the Faith, a moft gracious Prince, commiferating the deplorable ftate of things while the ruins were yet fmoking, provided for the comfort of his citizens and ornament of his city, remitted their taxes, and referred the petitions of the Magiftrates and inhabitants to the Parliament, who immediately paffed an Act that public works fhould be reftored to a greater beauty with public money, to be raifed by an impofition on coals; that Churches and the Cathedral of St. Paul fhould be rebuilt from their foundation with all magnificence; that bridges, gates, and prifons fhould be new made, the fhores cleanfed, the ftreets made ftraight and regular, fuch as were fteep levelled, and thofe too narrow made wider, and markets and fhambles removed to feparate places.   They alfo enacted that every houfe fhould be built with party walls, and all in front raifed of equal height, and thofe walls all of fquared ftone or brick, and that no man fhould delay building beyond the fpace of feven years. Moreover, care was taken to prevent all fuits about their bounds; alfo anniverfary prayers were enjoined, and to perpetuate the memory hereof to pofterity they caufed this Column to be erected.

"The work was carried on with diligence; London is reftored; but it is uncertain whether with greater fpeed or beauty.   A three years' time finifhed what was fuppofed to be the bufinefs of an age."

Round the bafe of the pillar are thefe words, erafed out by King James II's. order, but after the Revolution deeply engraven.

" This Pillar was fet up in perpetual remembrance of the moft dreadful burning of this Proteftant City, begun and carried on by the treachery of the Popifh Faction, in the beginning of September, in the year of our Lord 1666, in order to the carrying on [of] their horrid plot for extirpating the Proteftant religion and Englifh liberties, and introducing Popery and Slavery." [1]

Over the door is an infcription denoting the Mayors while it was building. I did not go into it, as I was informed the iron gallery was rotten. About a week before I came to London, a filly man, who got a denial from his Miftrefs, threw himfelf off the top of the Monument, and the people who took him up made a great deal of money by fhewing his brains and bruifes to the common people.

As I was taking particular notice of this beautiful pillar, we by chance faw an acquaintance pafs on the other fide, who afked us to walk

---

[1] This paragraph has been collated with Stow. ed. 1720, book ii., p. 181.

with him; and, having paffed through many
ftreets, [I] was furprifed when he, turning about,
afked me if I knew where I was. I replied I did
not know the name of the ftreet. He faid we
were on a bridge. I immediately recollected
this bridge; I had heard fo much of it. There
are but three vacancies from whence you can
have a profpect of the river and the innumerable
quantity of veffels, which form a foreft farther
than the eye can reach. Thefe openings are
guarded by iron pallifades. There are nineteen
arches under this bridge, and four of them are
employed or taken up by a huge engine, which
raifes the water to fupply the city. The repairs
of this machine and the bridge fometimes coft
the city three thoufand pounds per annum, and
it caufes the rent to come heavy on the inhabitants, who are compenfated by a brifk bufinefs,
which is commonly ftirring here.

The bridge was upwards of thirty years in
building. The river Thames is a fine river,
partly in the form of a crefcent, and widening in
the bent. There are very convenient fteps or
ftairs all round, attended by a vaft number of
fmall boats, which conftantly attend, and are
very ufeful when you are to go far.

From hence I was obliged to go to the Rainbow Coffee Houfe in Cornhill, to meet a friend by appointment, where my fatisfaction was increafed by receiving a letter from home, that informed me of all friends being well, and fome ftrange news concerning fome actions of a particular friend of mine, which I could not credit, 'till I confidered the fincerity of the perfon who wrote.

When dinner was over, I went to Spitalfields to finifh fome bufinefs, where I was detained till night. On my return Valerius told me with the greateft fpirits to haften to bed, "for," fays he, "we are to go to the Tower to-morrow, where the lions are kept, which I would rather fee than all the curiofities of London." I told him he might[1] ftay with the lions while we vifited the other parts of the Tower, thereby to take better notice of them. He faid, With all his heart, and foon went to bed. The next day, according to appointment, we all fet out on foot for the Tower, where after a tedious walk we arrived. It confifts of many old buildings, and withinfide the walls are upwards of fifty houfes (making a Parifh by itfelf), where the officers belonging to the Tower refide. We entered firft under a poftern on the fouth fide, where are[2] the apartments

---

[1] MS. has *may.*   [2] MS. has *is.*

for the lions and other favage beafts, kept in dens
railed to the front, which are divided into two
parts for the convenience of driving the beaft
into one while the other is cleaning.   The keeper
aroufed a lionefs, who was fo well trained that he
put his hand to her paw,[1] and [fhe] leaped over a
ftick, when, after fhe had performed, [fhe] lay
quietly down.   There were many young lions who
lolled in the dens.   We afterwards came to an
old lion (who had been there upwards of fixty
years), who feemed very compofed, but the man
putting in the pole, [he] fnapt at it, and made a
prodigious yelling.   From hence we went to a
parcel of uncommon large birds, and afterwards
to the panthers, leopards, and tigers ; the fkin of
the leopards is the moft beautifully mottled I
ever faw.   We entered next into a lofty room,
wherein were two oftriches (the largeft of
the bird kind) ; they are above nine feet high,
with beaks refembling a goofe['s] ; from the thigh
to the claw is much like a horfe, and the breadth
of the claw a foot and a half ; their necks are upwards of four foot long.   Thefe are but newly
come here, being a prefent made the laft fummer
by the Algerines, together with a young lion.

---

[1] MS. feems to read *Iaw*, but the writer probably omitted
to complete the firft letter—a *P.*

Valerius was particularly pleafed with thefe uncommon beafts, and accordingly furveyed 'em
attentively, and recorded what he faw in a pocket-
book he bought for that purpofe, and to which I
fhall refer the curious for a fuller information.
He meafured many of the beafts, and hath fet
down their different colours with vaft exactnefs.
He was near ten days in completing this little
treatife, which he intended for the amufement of
his friends, and would fet it forth under this
title, viz., " A Particular Survey of the Lions,
and feveral other uncommon Beafts and Birds of
Prey, as they are now in his Majefty's Tower
at London." I will venture to vouch for the
performance, as I am fenfible he fpared neither
time nor pains both in collecting the requifite materials and in putting it together with the utmoft
accuracy; and indeed I think our accounts hitherto
of them are but very defective, which will render
this of infinite fatisfaction. His readers muft
excufe him in not being particular in the length
of the old lion, who was really too fierce to be
meafured. From hence we went to fee the regalia, or repofitory of the jewels, and, entering a
dark cellar, [we] were[1] placed before an iron grate,
behind which a woman entered with a couple of

---

[1] MS. has *was*.

candles, and fhowed us all the curiofities, of which fhe gave me a bill, which, as it is fuller than any other account I can give, [I] have here inferted.

" A lift of his majefty's regalia, befides plate and other rich things at the jewel-houfe in the Tower of London.

1ft. The imperial crown, that all the kings of England have been crowned with from the time of Edward the Confeffor.

2d. The orb or globe held in the king's left hand at the coronation, on the top of which is a jewel near an inch and a half in height.

3d. The fceptre with the dove, the emblem of peace.

4. The royal fceptre with the crofs, which has another jewel of great value under it.

5. St. Edward's ftaff, all beaten gold, carried before the king at his coronation.

6. A rich falt-cellar of ftate, the figure of the Tower, ufed on the king's table at the coronation.

7. Curtana, or the fword of mercy, borne between the two fwords of juftice, fpiritual and temporal.

8. A noble filver font, double gilt, that the royal family are chriftened in.

9. A large filver fountain, prefented to king Charles the Second by the town of Plymouth.

10. The rich crown of ftate his majefty wears on his throne in Parliament, in which is a large emerald feven inches round, a pearl (the fineft in the world), and a ruby of ineftimable value.

11. His royal highnefs the Prince of Wales's crown.

12. Queen Mary's crown, globe, and fceptre, with the diadem fhe wore in proceeding to her coronation.

13. An ivory fceptre, with a dove, made for the late King James his queen.

14. The golden fpurs and the armillas worn at the coronation.

15. The ampulla or eagle of gold, which holds the holy oil the kings and queens of England are anointed with, and the golden fpoon the bifhop pours the oil into, which are great pieces of antiquity."

I received this bill when I had feen all the particulars therein mentioned, which was quite different from all the ordinaries I had ever feen, for the bill of fare is commonly produced before the meat is ferved up.

The woman handed me the fpurs, which fhe bid me put on my foot, which having done, fhe faid there was a forfeit thereunto belonging, which [1] I was obliged to pay.

[1] MS. has *and which.*

When I came out from this place, I viewed a
noble pile of building commonly called the Armoury, being upwards of four hundred feet in
length. At one end of it is the Spanifh Armoury,
fo called, as all the arms are here which we took
from the Spaniards at the time we burnt their
invincible Armada (as it was ftyled by the Pope),
and I verily believe they were certain of making
us flaves, as a vaft number of different kinds of
fetters and manacles are here fhown, with which
they intended to have bound us. The very fight
of thefe engines of flavery fhould be enough to
make us guard againft any fuch future attempt.
Here is an old axe, which 'tis faid beheaded
Queen Anne Bullen.

From hence we went to the Artillery Armoury, which takes up the entire length of this
long building on the ground. Here are the different kinds of warlike engines, and a great
number of light cannon ready mounted, the
larger fort being kept in the king's ftores in
Deptford, Woolwich, Portfmouth, &c.; as alfo
a great number of mortars of all fizes. There are
tackling and harneffes for feveral hundred[s] of
horfes, fo regularly difpofed and in good order
that they are ready at a minute's warning. I faw
the field-pieces the Duke of Cumberland had

with him at the Battle of Culloden in the late rebellion.[1] Here are many curious pieces of different invention, particularly one with nine barrels; alfo the firft great gun that was caft in England. In one corner ftands a well wrought brafs cannon, known by the name of Queen Anne's Pocket Piftol, and at the other fide two fmall pieces with which his prefent majefty was taught the art of gunnery. The upward part of this room is hung with a great number of pieces which were taken from the grand firework exhibited on the conclufion of the peace.

Our curiofity being fatisfied here, we were conducted next to the Horfe Armoury, wherein are the equeftrian ftatues of moft of the kings from Edward the Third to King William. At the door is placed King Henry the Eighth a-foot, with a pincufhion on his fleeve, wherein the ladies commonly ftick a pin, in return of which they are fhown another, though fomewhat of larger dimenfions. We went round a long paffage, where are placed on either fide a great number of coats of mail, among which is that of John of Gaunt (*fic*),[2] the French general, with the fword taken from him by Lord Kingfale (being

[1] MS. has *in the late rebellion at the Battle of Culloden.*

[2] See *Notes.*

fix foot long), for which exploit he was honoured
by being admitted to wear his hat in the prefence
of his majefty, which privileges his fucceffors as
yet retain.

We entered next the foot, or armoury of fmall
arms (of the fame fize as[1] the artillery armoury),
exceeding almoft defcription.   It is compofed
of mufkets, carbines, cutlaffes, bayonets, and
piftols.   There is a long walk on either fide,
with fluted columns of pikes, and in the pan[n]els
are feveral devices, fuch as the front of an organ,
waves of the fea in cutlaffes, fwords, and bayonets, funs with circles of piftols, a pair of gates
in halberts and piftols, the backbone of a whale
in carbines, the form of a battery in fwords and
piftols, a folding door, &c.; but what is moft
ftriking are the four columns wreathed with piftols, which rife to the top.   The middle is called
the Foreft of Guns, and there is enough to arm
an hundred thoufand men, all regularly placed,
divided in the infide with narrow paffages, where
they can eafily be got at; and what makes it
moft furprifing is that any fingle gun, piftol, and
any of the other arms, may be taken down without difturbing the next to it.   There are a great
number of fmiths conftantly employed in keep-
ing them clean.

[1] MS. has *of that of the.*

This grand piece of invention is not to be paralleled by any fuch in the univerfe, as all the ambaffadors of the different nations yield it the precedence, and what is more remarkable, 'tis the invention of one Harris, a poor blackfmith, who had a large penfion granted him when he completed it.

A little below the armoury ftands a fquare building with a turret on each angle, called the White Tower, wherein[1] they fay are upwards of two hundred thoufand mufkets and their accoutrements, though not placed in the beautiful manner above mentioned, but [they] are ready if occafion ferved. In this tower are kept records and other law affairs.

My curiofity would have been entirely fatisfied, could I have feen the Mint, which is fomething difficult, as they do not choofe to fhow it to ftrangers; it was near four o'clock by the time we had feen all the curiofities afforded by the Tower, which fufpended my appetite, while they were before me, but it recurred when I had loft thefe inviting objects; which haftened us away. We were quite indifferent about the place of dining, refolving to take up the firft [which] fhould offer, and I believe we walked upwards of a mile,

[1] MS. has *and wherein.*

inquiring at every fourth houfe for dinner, but
as the time was paft, we could not be fupplied.
I made an odd reflection on this kind of treatment, viz., that we were in the fineft city in
Europe, had money in our pocket, and could
get nothing to eat. At length we got into an
indifferent houfe, where we bought fome lobfters,
which, with fome falad and cold meat, made a
comfortable dinner, of which we eat very heartily,
efpecially Valerius who, I believe, had gained an
uncommon ftomach by converfing fo long with
the lions, &c., who have naturally an infatiable
appetite. I will not fay whether it was in imi-
tation of his favourites or not, but I felt the
effects of it, for the lobfters difappeared of a
fudden.

It was near five o'clock by the time we finifhed
this laft diverfion. My father propofed going
to Cuper's Gardens. Indeed, my thoughts were
fo wholly taken up with the Tower that I made
fome objection to it, but as he again mentioned
it, and Valerius, being ever attentive to novelty,
urged it fo clofe, I[1] found it impoffible to refufe. We provided a boat, and in lefs than an
hour got thither, but were difappointed, as there
was no performance this night. As the evening

[1] MS. has *that I.*

was very calm, and the beautiful proſpect afforded
by the river and the buildings contiguous to it
made us ſtay a long while on the water, we went
to the new bridge at Weſtminſter, and ſailed
under ſeveral of the arches. This bridge hath
been lately built by ſubſcription and taxes on
coal, and is the fineſt in Europe. The middle
arch is ſixty foot wide, and the reſt decreaſe in
the juſt proportion, being ſeventeen in number.
'Tis of Portland ſtone, finely wrought, and riſes
to a vaſt height in the centre. On the top is a
ſpacious way for carriages, and the ſides [are] neatly
flagged for foot-paſſengers. The wall riſes about
ſix feet, above which are rails hewn with great
art, through which you have an extenſive proſpect of the river and boats.

We did not return till night, and I was much
better pleaſed in viewing this noble bridge than
[with] all the amuſements afforded by the gardens.
We reſolved the next day to viſit the Abbey of
Weſtminſter. We had not breakfaſted when a
coach waited for us at the door, into which we
ſoon hurried, and at length [were] ſet down at
this truly awful and noble building.

The length of it is near five hundred feet; the
choir is in the middle, and the aiſles ſurround it,
in which are placed many beautiful monuments;

the best worth viewing are the Duke of Newcastle's
Sir Isaac Newton's at the west end of the choir,
Mr. Secretary Craggs, &c. These are esteemed
the grandest by connoisseurs in architecture, but
I think there are many which strike the eye as
agreeably. The Poets chiefly lie at the west end
of the Abbey, and have handsome monuments,
with inscriptions *à propos* to the genius of him
who is interred. I shall set down a few of 'em
as they are placed :—Gay, Rowe, Shakespeare,
Shadwell, Milton, Prior, Butler, Ben Jonson,
J. Dryden. I stood some time buried in thought
and contemplation on viewing the place where these
great men lay, who, though [they] had here but a
few stones erected to their memories, yet had left
behind them immortal monuments, which can
reach to the remotest nation ; whereas the stately
tombs which are set up to a Duke at vast expense
lie confined amongst these walls, and can afford
no other satisfaction than that of admiring the
work of the artist, when perhaps we hardly know
the name of him who is therein. But the monument of a genius is everywhere dispersed, and
gives us a deep sense of the loss ; which, I believe,
was the original intent of this kind of building,
when they would remember a man who had been
of signal service ; but the meaning is lost, because

every blockhead who has money can have one raifed.

The Chapel of King Henry the Seventh is curious, as it is filled with many fine monuments of the kings and queens who have been buried there. His own is very grand, and is enriched with many ftatues, &c. On the eaft fide are two Cupids fupporting an imperial crown. There are abundance of other devices and infcriptions, which had I been particular in, [I] muft have come [for] fome weeks. The roof, which is all ftone, is divided into fixteen circles, curioufly wrought, and is the admiration of all who fee it. The outfide of the Abbey makes but an odd appearance, the ftone being formerly hewn, but at prefent fo much decayed and mouldered away, [that it] makes it look the more ancient.

Having paft the moft folemn and agreeable day, we took our places in the coach, and returned at about five o'clock. I was fo ftruck with the antiquities afforded by the Abbey that I believe I was fo entirely buried in contemplation the whole night that I fpoke not at all.

The next day I went to the common place of rendezvous (the Exchange), where I accidentally met with a man with whom Valerius had an acquaintance. He was no other than the

R

fprightly Phædrus, who feldom failed of diverting thofe with whom he met, and, though he
was not a man of folidity, yet I concluded our
journey would be made perfectly agreeable between Valerius and him.[1]   We concluded to take
the ftage on Monday following for Briftol, in
which Phædrus faid he would likewife go.   It
being now Friday, 'twas high time to prepare for
our departure, and accordingly we packed up the
next morning moft of our baggage.   When we
had fettled moft of our affairs at this end of the
town, we fent for a coach, and by the time it
arrived found ourfelves in a readinefs to embark.
We fet out, defiring the man to drive to the
One Bell in[2] the Strand, near the new Church.
As this is near St. James's, we thought it the beft
to pafs the remainder of our ftay there, as we
fhould have been obliged to come[3] thither, becaufe the Briftol ftage fets out from thence.

We viewed moft part of this end of the town
after dinner, and from thence we went into the
park, where I walked above two hours.   This is
an extreme fine park, furrounded by three level
walks, planted with well grown trees, which[4] in

---

[1] MS. has *be*. The name is unqueftionably *Phædrus*, but
the writer or copyift, except when he firft introduces him,
always fpells the word (phonetically) *Phadrus*.

[2] MS. has *on*.   [3] MS. has *have come*.   [4] MS. has *and*.

the middle of fummer in great heats afford a very
refrefhing fhelter. Round the infide walk are
long feats where people may reft themfelves.
Thefe walks are crowded in the evening with a
great quantity of ladies and gentlemen, who can
entertain each other, and receive a double benefit,
that of the air and converfation. In the middle
of the park is a long regular canal, upon which
are a number of wild ducks belonging to His
Majefty.

At my return to the One Bell I found my
father had engaged places for himfelf and me;
Phædrus had alfo taken one, and three others,
which of confequence left no room for Valerius,
who was mightily difpleafed, and was obliged
to be content in travelling with the coachman.

Next day being Sunday, I refolved once again
to vifit the Abbey of Weftminfter, and accordingly got up fome time earlier, and walked round
moft of the aifles before the fervice began.
When it was over, Valerius and I took two or
three turns on the park, and on our return to the
fquare found my father, who faid we muft go to
fee the Prince of Wales return from Chapel.
We then walked to the Palace, which is an old
building on the north fide of the park, but I

believe never was intended for the refidence of a
monarch; it makes but a wretched appearance,
looking not much better than a heap of dead
walls. We afcended by a large ftaircafe to a
long room, through which the royal family were
to pafs. This was Prince George's birthday, who
came from his country feat (Kew) to receive the
compliments of the nobility, a number of which
were continually paffing into the drawing-room.
I placed myfelf in a very advantageous pofture,
and had remained near half an hour, when they
came out of chapel. Prince George entered
firft (who this day entered into his fourteenth
year), and, though in fo tender years, he difcovered all the marks of manlinefs, his action
quite free and unconfined; an innocent fmile
played upon his countenance while he bowed to
the throng that environed him, and he feemed no
way attentive to the glittering fhow that furrounded him. In a word, a princely dignity
betrayed itfelf in the moft undefigning of his
actions, and gives us the greateft hopes of his
filling the throne in as confpicuous a manner as
his noble progenitors. Certainly, 'tis impoffible
to look at him and not love him. Princefs
Amelia came afterwards with Prince Edward,
followed by the Duke of Cumberland.

We waited about half an hour till their return, when I had a fecond opportunity of feafting my eyes on the Prince, who got into his hand chair, attended by the battle-axes through a regiment of guards which waited on him.

A public clock had juft ftruck five when we came down. I found my ftomach at the ftair-foot, but was much difheartened, as the time of the day gave me no hopes of getting a meal[1] fpeedily; neverthelefs we happened into a very good houfe, the mafter of which was an Irifhman, by which means we got the better fare; for he foon ferved up fome French foup [and] a goofe, and provided us a bottle of excellent wine; and indeed it was a rarity, as I had tafted none good fince my coming to England.

After dinner I walked to the park, where I faw an incredible number of ladies and fafhions. Valerius made fome pretty remarks on them, which I am in hopes of his inferting with his Treatife on the Lions, otherwife I fhould have endeavoured to have done his remarks juftice by committing them to paper; but as I know his ability more capable in things of this nature, and as[2] I am in hopes of his purfuing his intention, I have here omitted it.

[1] MS. has *one*.   [2] MS. has *that*.

At dufk we returned to the One Bell, where we put everything in readinefs for our departure next morning. Phædrus came in lefs than an hour afterwards with his portmanteau. We made a light fupper and went to bed early, as we were told we muft be up at two o'clock, at which hour the chamber-maid aroufed us. Having got a bottle of white wine and a twopenny bun, in a few minutes my Father, Phædrus and I got into the coach, and Valerius mounted the box; and he very wittily[1] remarked, that though the generality of people efteemed the body of the coach moft honourable, yet he would fuftain that in many parts in tragedy the heroes are diftinguifhed by being placed on an eminence, one of which he would now imagine himfelf.

Though my ftay in London was fo fhort, yet I faw abundance of other beautiful buildings, [befides] them here inferted; but as thefe are the moft remarkable, [I] thought I could not well difpenfe with[2] giving at leaft a curfory defcription of them.

Our coach went on as faft as the pavements would admit, and when we had received many fevere jolts, we ftopped at a houfe, at which our coachman bellowed. The door was immediately

---

[1] MS. has *wittingly*.　　　[2] MS. has *without*.

opened, and foon prefented us with three females, who[m] I could not well difcern, it being as yet dark. I heard one of them cry out in a peevifh, affected tone, "Lord, how many have you got in the coach?" to which I replied, putting my head out of the window, that we would endeavour to make room for the ladies. She made no anfwer but that it did not fignify complaining, but that fhe was a fool for not taking another place in the coach. The ladies placed themfelves with the profoundeft filence, not even making an anfwer to the many compliments I made them. I could obferve, though it was dark, that one of them was young. This made me conjecture that the woman who fpoke was a governefs or mother to the young one. I refolved to be filent till I could gather more, and was very timorous of difobliging her, left it might[1] be a conftraint on the young one. I endeavoured to gain her good opinion by feveral civilities that I could invent, fuch as offering her my feat, and preffing her to tafte the wine, which with fome difficulty I perfuaded her to. As we had no converfation to enliven us, moft of us took a nod till we arrived at Slough to breakfaft. When the coach ftopped, I leaped out to hand out my particular,

[1] MS. has *may*.

but oh, ye who are martyrs to love ! judge of my aſtoniſhment when I received in my hand an old withered ſpectre, ſcarce worth accounting amongſt the living. She ſeemed to be one of the old caſt miſtreſſes, who for reaſons travel up and down the country. She appeared to have an opinion of herſelf which I dare ſay was different from mine; but before I venture to give her my heart I think it will not be amiſs to give ſome deſcription of an object which indeed for a great while attracted my admiration.

She had a long viſage, which ſeemed battered from the effects of time ; her head was banded or ſwathed up in exquiſite taſte; two red eyes ſtood buried in their hollow orbs, and endeavoured (I believe) to diſplay the remains of ſome arts ſhe had learned in her juvenile days; her noſe ſeemed ſomething like a ſickle, from whence diſtilled a certain denſe liquid, which I concluded to proceed from the immoderate uſe of a certain pulverized Indian weed, the effuſion of which very gracefully ſettled or remained on her upper lip, overflowing a thicket of hair which ſpontaneouſly grew there. Her chin, ſhamed into good manners by the politeneſs of her noſe, alſo made its advances, forming together half an oval. I was ſo buried in contemplating this beauty that it deprived me of the proper function which fhould have employed me, for fhe ftumbled againft a large ftone, which made her open a wide mouth entirely deftitute of utenfils to bemoan the accident. I could not but admire the graceful manner of her utterance.

The young woman did not prove entirely to my liking, and, as in our difcourfe at breakfaft her companions addreffed her by the title of Mrs., I refolved not to lofe the time with the old dame, as I knew I could take all the freedoms allowed by that ftate.

I made as much acquaintance with the young one as to afk her, was the old lady married. She replied fhe never was. This information did not difpleafe me. When I handed her to the coach, I knew the point [which] would moft pleafe her, and accordingly launched out on her praifes with a thorough contempt on all coxcombs ; and, when I had an opportunity, introduced a joke on matrimony. She expreffed a great abhorrence of it, faying no young woman fhould throw away her youth in it. She would admit of no joke except them which could not offend the ear of a Platonift. She was indeed one of thefe old precife maids who, having fpent all their lives and art in endeavouring to get an hufband, and finding their

efforts too weak, refolve to exclaim againft every
tittle of it, to bring themfelves off with credit in
feeming to refufe what they would willingly accept.   On my credit, I pitied her, and refolved,
inftead of adding to her misfortunes, to foothe
and comfort her. I behaved in the moft obliging
manner poffible, paying her the deference.   We
had now got on Hounflow Heath, a long piece of
wafte or untilled ground, which[1] is commonly infefted with robbers. Phædrus told many dreadful
ftories of them, which I knew he did out of arch-
nefs to affright the old lady.

We paffed this morning by many fine feats,
particularly Kew (the Prince of Wales's) and
Windfor Palace, finely fituated on a hill.   The
country all around, covered with villas, makes
the moft agreeable landfcape imaginable.

At one we got to Reading, an indifferent town,
but watered all round by many rivulets and
brooks, and [I] believe we paffed over more than
half a dozen wooden bridges, which lead to the
town. We found an excellent dinner here, which
having finifhed, we proceeded on our journey,
and paffed through many agreeable villages till
we came to Newbury.

This is [a] pretty regular town, well built, about

[1] MS. has *and.*

fixty miles from London, and the river Thames is made navigable up here by means of a deep canal, which coft an immenfe fum ; but I am apt to think the projeét anfwered the expeétation and expenfe, for large flat-bottom boats of an hundred and fifty ton can come fo far up[1] the country and drop their freight in the feveral parts as they pafs. They generally are loaded back with grain and fuch commodities as are to be fold in the city. This contrivance is of great ufe, as it makes the carriage exceeding cheap, as four horfes can tow one of them with eafe.

Moft of the company were affembled to fupper when I returned from this ramble,[2] but I was furprifed when the other two women told us the old lady was gone to bed, adding, by the bye, that it was to fave expenfe. All the good opinion I before entertained of her vanifhed, and made room for a kind of antipathy which I could not refift, as I thought fhe had hitherto no reafon to complain of the gentle treatment fhe had received from us. I could form no other fuppofition than that fhe feared fhe would be made to pay. Phæ-

---

[1] MS. has *up in*. The Thames had been made navigable fo far as Oxford in 1715.

[2] Something feems to be wanting in the MS., as the narrative is evidently not quite confecutive.

drus fwore he would be revenged of her, and for
that purpofe made a friend of the chambermaid,
who promifed to fhow us to a couple of beds
adjoining to the old lady's chamber.|

Supper being over, we went to our room,
which was divided but by a thin partition. Phædrus and Valerius lay together.   They were no
fooner in bed than they begun a violent fcreaming,
which I thought would have aroufed the houfe,
beating time by driving their fhoes at the wain-
fcot.   They[1] continued fo till one o'clock, when
with much difficulty I begged them to let us
have one hour's fleep, which they[2] complied with ;
but I fhould have been better pleafed to have been
awake the remainder of the time we were to ftay;
and I hardly knew I was afleep when I was
ftartled by the fcreaming of a maid at my chamber
door, who bellowed forth the coach was ready,
which I heard echoed from the yard by the hoarfe
voice of the coachman, with a b——d and n——s
he would not wait.   This gentle alar[u]m aroufed
my drowzy fpirits, when I fprung from the downy
abode (though, by the bye, I believe it was flocks,
for I do not remember to have had fo hard a bed
fince I came to England).

When we got to the yard we found the women

[1] MS. has *Hc.*   [2] MS. has *be.*

ready to embark, and when we were feated, Phædrus wifhed the ladies a good morning, and hoped
they had repofed well the fmall time [which] was
allowed them. The other two, who were ignorant
of our midnight tranfactions, replied in the affirmative, but, alas! the old dame, opening her mouth,
faid fhe believed there were not fuch another pack
of people in the world, " for," added fhe, " I have
not got a wink of fleep all night." Phædrus
feemed mightily furprifed, and was impatient to
know the caufe, and added that no one dare dif-
turb her while he had the honour of her company. She faid fhe wifhed fhe could have lefs of
his, for fhe never was fo ufed before, for that
fhe had the misfortune to be in the next room.
Phædrus innocently replied that it was impoffible,
for he faw the other ladies going to the other
end of the houfe. She anfwered difdainfully that
as fhe was no lady, fhe fuppofed that was the
reafon they put her by fuch ruffians. Phædrus,
putting on a very fubmiffive countenance, thus
addreffed his fair :—

" How unjuftly you accufe me I fhall not fay,
as I am perfectly confcious of my own innocence.
Were I fenfible of the happinefs of your being in
the next room, be affured no confideration could
have tempted my tongue (which I am now ready

to ſacrifice to your diſpleaſure) to tranſgreſs in a point ſo inconſiſtent with my will. Let then, I beſeech you, this my ignorance plead pardon for a crime more foreign to my intent than London and Pekin. My future amendment will convince you of my repentance, which will, I hope, atone for my paſt miſconduct, and replace me in your favour."

Whether ſhe was ſo very ſtupid as not to comprehend this banter, or that ſhe thought it was her due, [I] ſhall not ſay, but ſhe relaxed in his favour, and ſaid all ſhe looked for was the performance, which would moſt effectually determine her in the good opinion he expected from her.

I could not avoid ſmiling how ridiculous ladies in her unhappy circumſtances often make themſelves; they think every body is bound to humour their caprice, and ſeldom take the pains of being agreeable to any one. The ſelfiſh opinion which they are commonly addicted to commonly diſapproves of anything that does not favour according to their taſte. I have indeed the luck of being acquainted with one or two of this caſt, but, as I am no ſtranger to the diſappointments they have met with, I am inclined to make the greateſt allowances for the want of temper and

fprightlinefs which misfortunes of this kind rarely
fail of producing.

Matters being thus adjufted, we paffed the
morning very agreeably. Phædrus fung many
witty airs, and took more than uncommon care of
pleafing the lady; and he managed his part with
fo much dexterity that fhe began to practife over
fome of her airs, which fhe thought would retain
her conqueft. About nine o'clock we were fet
down at Marlborough, no way remarkable but
for the cleannefs of it, where we breakfafted,
when the ladies informed us they were to quit us
five miles of the place we fhould dine at. Phædrus feemed much affected with this piece of
news, and afked if it was not poffible for them to
go to Bath.

We took our places in the coach, and foon
after got on a large common called Marlborough
Downs: the coach ftopped, and the driver fhowed
us fome large grey ftones, called the Grey Wea-
thers. They grow out of the earth, and fome of
the inhabitants have remembered them to grow
fome feet. On this plain is a huge pile of earth,
taper-wife, formerly one of the Danes' forts. I
have feen many of the fame form in Ireland, but
none any way comparable in fize to this.

Phædrus feemed mightily caft down, and

looked[1] for fome time wifhfully on his miftrefs.
After he had obferved a profound filence for fome
time, he at length broke out into this fpeech with
a ferioufnefs that furprifed me.

" 'Tis of no purpofe," faid he, addreffing himfelf to her, " you endeavour to hide what your
looks and geftures fo manifeftly difcover. I have
obferved, fince I firft had the pleafure of feeing
you, that you have regarded me with more than
uncommon civility. Pray, what could be the
meaning of having me feated by you at table and
helping me to the daintieft morfels, with feveral
circumftances of the like obliging nature? For
my part, there is no fin in the univerfe I deteft fo
much as ingratitude, were there no other motive
for me to be interefted ; but, when I find the advantage entirely fall on my fide, can I be fo re-
markably ftupid as to let flip advantages which I
venture to fay would be preferred by numbers as
the only happinefs of their lives ?"

As this was uttered in fo grave a tone, I will
not avouch whether fhe believed it or not, tho'
fhe feemed quite ftartled at it, and faid fhe did
not underftand his meaning. To which he anfwered with the fame continued ferioufnefs,—
" Had I fpoke in much obfcurer terms to a per-

[1] MS. has *looking*.

fon of your apprehenfion on any other topic, I am
convinced you would have underftood me; but,
fince my ftyle muft have an interpretation which
your modefty will not permit you to underftand,
to fpeak in a few words, I perceive you are in
love with me, and have been fo fince you faw me.
'Tis in vain to deny it—nay, do not, for, as I am all
fubmiffion, and willing to make you happy, let's
not longer delay our blifs." At which words he
ftopped the coachman, and afked him how far it
was to the next clergyman. He replied, " Not
above a mile." Phædrus faid he would requite
him if he dropped him there, upon which Valerius (underftanding the joke), leaped from the
coachbox, and fwore he would run before and
prepare the clergyman, to prevent delay. The
old lady feemed very much furprifed at this kind
of proceeding, and really imagined he intended
going for the parfon, though I believe fhe began
to comprehend the banter, and, refolving to be
revenged of the affront, faid to Valerius that he
was an unmannerly jackanapes, and, was it worth
her while, [fhe] would have him punifhed at the
next town. The gravity and fret fhe uttered this
with made me laugh, fpite of all my efforts to
the contrary. Poor Valerius was greatly out of
countenance, and crept up to his box.

It would feem ridiculous to fpin this jeft to a greater length, and I believe I fhould not have mentioned it had I any.hing more material to fupply its place. The country, indeed, may ferve for a nobler topic, but, as I have defcr ebed it more than once, fo many repetitions may feem ftupid.

At length we got to the place where our ladies departed from us, w'thout much regret on either fide. The old lady, as we fet off, faid fhe hoped fhe never would meet [again] with fuch a wild Irifhman as Phædrus.

Their departure made room for Valerius,[1] who immediate' y took his place, but I believe he would have wifhed to be in his old place, becaufe he fuffered fo much from our railleries. About one we got to Sandy Lane, where we dined. This place derives its name from itfelf, being a long lane of deep fand, which annoys travellers on windy days, but not in fo difmal a manner as the fandy defert of Arabia, which frequently buries fome thoufands of people in their pilgrimage to Mecca. There is but one houfe here, but good accommodations, and you[2] commonly find at dinner

---

[1] MS. has *Phædrus*, although, juft half a page before, the writer informed us that it was *Valerius*, who took the boxfeat.   [2] MS. has *we.*

a particular kind of a pudding, which is very good, well known over moſt parts of England by the name of a Sandy Lane Pudding. Dinner being finiſhed, we proceeded on our journey, and at the end of this lane found a warren for rabbits, in which were the greateſt quantity I ever ſaw. Nothing worth remarking happened till we got to Bath about ſeven o'clock, and really I was well pleaſed to refreſh myſelf from the fatigue, as we intended to make ſome little ſtay here.

I was informed in London of a particular friend of mine, who came to Bath for the benefit of his health, and had brought all his family. While my father diſcharged the coach, I inquired out his lodgings, whither I ſent a note, and received anſwer that he would be glad to ſee us that night. I ſent an excuſe, but promiſed to breakfaſt with him next morning.

After a long and ſound ſleep I awakened exceedingly refreſhed, and by the time my father and I were prepared we found our friend's ſervant waiting to conduct us to his maſter's, who[m] we found but very indifferent. His lady received us with the greateſt civility, and ſoon after his daughter entered, with whom, as I had before ſeen her, we ſoon began to chat. When breakfaſt was over, ſhe conducted me to ſeveral hot baths, and

it furprifed me to find fome of them bubble as if
boiling, and fo warm as you could fcarce put
your hand in them. From hence we went to the
pump-room, where people affemble to chat and
drink the waters. I drank a few glaffes, but, indeed, they were of a very difagreeable flavour.
We proceeded next to the long room. It is a
well-built houfe, compofed of feveral rooms for
gaming, which they practife here to an immoderate degree. The dancing-rooms are well furnifhed, and in one of them is the portraiture of
Beau Nafh in full length. This is the man who
regulates all the affairs of this houfe, and fits pre-
fident in the feafon. There is a beautiful church
in this town, tho' not fo grand as fome already
defcribed, and a good market, well furnifhed,
tho' fometimes at an extravagant rate. We
walked round moft of the town, when we returned to dinner at three o'clock with our friend,
who infifted on it at breakfaft. The walk got
me a good appetite, and at dinner we were informed of a fhip that intended to fail the day
after next, which made us refolve to fet out for
Briftol next morning, being unwilling to mifs the
firft opportunity for Cork, tho' we intended to
have ftayed here longer. This unwelcome news
made me refolve to fee as much of the town as pof-

fible, and the young lady, though fo much tired
in the morning, infifted on fhowing it to me.
We traverfed all worth feeing of it, and I was
really charmed with the obliging manner and
the pains fhe took of informing me in what fhe
thought the moft neceffary. I fhould account
myfelf very ungrateful if I flipped any opportunity of doing juftice and acknowledging the
friendfhip and politenefs fhe difcovered to me.

At night I returned and took leave of my
friend, his lady, and his agreeable daughter, and,
having procured places in the coach, I took an
imaginary view of what I had feen this day, and
fhall endeavour to defcribe what I could recollect.

It is a large town, fituated on the declivity of
a hill on one fide : the ftreets are regularly built
of a freeftone which is found near, and cut or
hewn in great tafte : the ftreets are paved with a
fquare flag, and fo even as renders walking very
agreeable ; the Parade, or Beau-part of the town,
is built very grand, the houfes rifing a great
height, and the oppofite fide is fenced with ftone
palifades, through which you[1] have an enchanting
profpect of the feats and gardens of feveral no-
blemen. Withinfide is a large fquare, built after
the fame manner, and fenced round the houfes

[1] MS. has *we.*

with a rail, the fame as before mentioned, in the middle of which ftands a quadrangular pedeftal or fpire, terminating in a very fharp point, which[1] is called Beau Nafh's Toothpick. The length of one of thefe fquares is a noble building or apartment, known by the name of the Queen's Building, being the place where the royal family have refided, or refide in, when they come to the bath.

Next morning we again mounted the jolting machine, and got to Briftol about eleven o'clock. We fent our lumber to the quay,[2] where we took lodgings, as being the propereft for our purpofe. By the direction we found out the captain, who told us he was difappointed in his loading, and that he believed he could not fail thefe three days. I was much fretted at this account, as I could have ftayed longer in Bath without inconvenience, and to return again for fo fhort a time did not feem worth while. This evening happening to be wet, [I] could not ftir out of doors, but was obliged to take a book to pafs the remainder of the day.

Next morning I went on the quay, but was very much furprifed to find the river fo very muddy, which I concluded to proceed from the heavy rain that fell the night before, but on in-

---

[1] MS. has *and*.   [2] MS. has *key* here and *infrâ*.

quiry found it was continually fo. I can no
better give a juft idea of it than by a witty remark a young lady of my acquaintance made on
her firft feeing it, " That it feemed as if Nature
had taken a purge, and that was the operation."
The filth and dirt that floats on [the] top makes
it very loathfome. The quays here are of a prodigious height, becaufe the tide flows fo high,
and commonly with fuch rapidity that it furprifed
me. When it is quite ebbed, the mafts of the
fhips reach to the level of the quay, and the
landing of goods would be very difficult, were it
not for a number of cranes which are placed all
along it ; and it is worth obferving that one man
with the greateft eafe can raife a ton burden.
The bridge is made of timber, and, when any
fhip is to pafs, it opens in the middle by means
of an engine on either fide.

I went to the other fide of the bridge up a
hill to a place called College Green ; 'tis of a
triangular form, enclofed with wooden palifades,
and divided within into regular walks, which are
kept gravel'd and planted with well-grown trees,
kept in good order. In the middle is a fquare,
where all the walks terminate, wherein ftands a high
wooden monument or fpire, called High Crofs ;
it is fupported by five pillars, forming an arch

under. On the capitals are four niches, wherein
are placed as many ſtatues, cut in the Gothic
taſte, and above them as many more in a ſitting
poſture ; and from thence ariſes a ſpire, whereon
is a croſs. 'Tis well worth noticing, both for the
manner of carving and the age. This is ſaid to
have been[1] ſet up in King Richard the Third's
time in Redcliff Street, but afterwards removed
to the place [where] it now ſtands. There is a
large ſtreet without the rails all around, well built.

I went to the Exchange, very neat and well
built, modelled from the Royal Exchange in
London, but not near [that] as to the dimenſions
or grandeur of the pile. On the entrance is a
coffee houſe on one ſide, and a tavern on the
other. I was ſurpriſed to ſee moſt of the merchants aſſembled in the ſtreet, tranſacting their
affairs, and very few within. As the Exchange
hath been newly finiſhed, and the people never
before uſed to one, [they] cannot as yet reconcile
themſelves to it. The London merchants ſay,
" The Briſtol hogs have built a ſty, but cannot
find the way into it."

The next day happened to be the martyrdom
of King Charles the Firſt, and at my going out [I]
thought I was in a wood by the number of oaken

[1] MS. has *be.*

boughs hung at almoſt every door. The common people had ſprigs in their hats, and put 'em
in their horſes' heads. The Corporation here obſerve it as one of their ſtate days. I went to the
church, which is called the College Church,
whither they were to come, and had time to take
a particular view of it before their arrival.

There is a large aiſle about it with ſome
monuments. The ſervice part is very old, and
makes an odd figure with the variety of carving.
There is an indifferent choir, but a very good
organ.

This was formerly a ſeminary or college for
[the] educating of youth, and this church belonged
to it, the building extending at either ſide a great
length, and one of the old gates is now ſtanding,
very oddly carved.

The trades preceded the mayor and alder-
men with their reſpective colours, who afterwards
came in coaches with each a pair of gold-fringed
gloves. As the reſt of the ceremony was accompanied with ſome hurry, I retired to ſeek
my captain, who I thought would ſail on the
morrow, [but] who ſaid he had not yet got his
loading, but expected in three days more to be
able to go. Repining was of the leaſt ſervice,

and [I] reſolved to act the part of a philoſopher as much as poſſible.

The viewing of Brandon Hill and the Lead Houſe occupied the moſt part of the next day, whither we went under the conduct of a friend. This is a high lump of a hill, which commands an agreeable proſpect of the town and a great way into the country. On the ſummit are the ruins of ſome old caſtle or fort, but [I] could not learn by any tradition what it was. The hill was be-ſtowed [on] the city to dry clothes on by Queen Ann[e], and indeed it is naturally well adapted to the purpoſe, as I am told it conſtantly retains its verdure, and where you[1] ſeldom miſs of a ſharp drying wind. We deſcended to the White Lead Houſe, which lies at the foot of it, and, as we had a friend in it, he ſhewed us it very particu-larly. The omiſſion would ſeem too groſs if I did not endeavour to be as particular in the recital.

The ſmelting houſe, or place where they run the lead (into very thin plates about eight inches broad), is on the entrance. At one ſide ſtands the furnace where the metal is, and four men are kept conſtantly caſting the ſheets. When a great quantity of theſe ſheets are thus prepared, they are made up into rolls; each roll is afterwards

---

[1] MS. has *we.*

placed into an earthen pot, made for the purpofe;
a proper number of thefe pots being laid down,
[they] are filled up with very ftrong vinegar, afterwards are covered with planks, on which they fet
another row, and fo place planks again with
another layer of pots till they raife a high pile,
which is afterwards covered over with horfe-
dung. They lie in this manner feven or eight
weeks, when they are uncovered, and there remains on the lead a white fkin or film, occafioned
by the vinegar, which is entirely exhaufted.
They take the rolls out of the pots, and lay them
in order till they are quite dry, when they are
taken and put in a mill, which fcrapes or cleans
all the ftuff off which fticks to the lead. It is
afterwards ground in a mill with fair water, and
conducted from thence by fpouts into large
coolers, where it is again purified with water in
the following manner :—The coolers are more
than half filled with the lead, and the remaining
part is covered with water. They both are ftirred
together, and when it fettles for a while, the dirt
or filth fwims on the water, which is let out by
means of a large hole. The purified lead is
taken out and laid upon long beds of chalk,
divided into fquares about fix inches. When it
is perfectly dry, it is barrelled up and expofed to

fale. There are kinds differing according to their finenefs, but our painters in this kingdom (as I was told) feldom make ufe but of the coarfeft. 'Tis exceeding dangerous to work here becaufe of the duft that flies when the mill cleans it from the lead.

In the evening we went to a pretty garden near the Hot Wells, which they call Vauxhall. There are fome booths and pleafant arbours, hung with fome globe lamps, &c., [and] an orcheftra, wherein were a good band of mufic. There was no company here this night, which rendered it very difagreeable, and feveral times after but very few. The poor man who owned it was at a great expenfe to keep it in order, but in a fhort time after was obliged to decamp.

The next day it rained fo very much that it was impoffible to fet a foot out of doors, but the day after the dreary fcene changed to a fine day.

The next place I vifited was Queen Square. This is a large piece of ground lying on a flat, planted with large trees, with fpacious walks through it. The outfide hath many well-built houfes. On one fide of the Square is the Cuftom Houfe, no way grand, but very convenient for the purpofe.

My impatience to get from this place hurried

me to the Exchange at the ufual hour, when, on
inquiring of the Captain, he told me he would
not fail in a week. Any ftranger who hath ever
been in this place can judge how agreeable it is
to be here, as the people fhew the leaft hof-
pitality or affection for any one who[m] they do
not expect to be a gainer by. As my ftay was
long here, I vifited many places about the town.
I often went to the Hot Wells, much refembling
the Bath waters. Here is a good room for dancing.
King's Down is a high piece of ground on the
other fide of the town from Brandon Hill.
There is a fine inland profpect from it and of the
greater part of the town. I faw many glafs
houfes, with which this town vaftly abounds,
as the inhabitants reckon upwards of thirty.
The generality of them are built of brick, taper-
wife to the top. Withinfide is the chaldron
wherein the metal is boiled by the means of a large
conftant fire with a chimney, by which the fmoke
is conveyed through the top. There are holes all
around the furnace, through which they take the
metal. I faw feveral things blown. This is
performed by a long iron tube, the end of which
they dip into the metal, and after they have given
it a blaft or two, they form or fhape it on an
anvil. It would require fome nicety to give a

fuccinct account of the preparation of the metal and the other branches belonging to glafs work.

Redcliff church is the beft worth viewing of any in Briftol. This is a noble old ftructure, built of Portland or freeftone. The tower is very ftrong, in which is a fine peal of eight bells, accounted the largeft in the town. We entered by a noble aifle, the roof fupported by grand fluted pillars ; the ceiling is very beautiful, adorned with variety of carving. Here are fome monuments, particularly that of a pirate, by whom 'tis faid the church was built. The tradition runs thus :—

This pirate infefted the feas for a long while, and thereby gained an immenfe fortune, fpite of all the veffels which were employed by the Government to prevent him. At length, being wearied by continually avoiding them that were fent to take him, he petitioned his Majefty for a pardon, which was granted thus :—" That he fhould have his life the length of time that he would take in building a church, but that he muft not omit to work any day." He accepted it on thefe conditions, and, to render it the longer, 'tis faid he would not let a beaft draw any of the materials, but [the work] was entirely performed by men.

I fhall not take upon me to aver this for

fact, but any body who reads it will have the same choice as I had when it was told to me, to believe it or not.

The choir is extremely handsome and paved throughout with marble; over the altar-piece is a grand window, glazed (except a little), with stained glass.

Bristol, indeed, may boast a great number of good buildings; the town is situated partly between two hills, and is refreshed by a good air, which blows from off the country side. The town itself is but disagreeable; the streets are generally dirty and close built, except a few which lie from the main body; but what contributes more to its disadvantage is the muddy river which flows in it, and this circumstance, in my single opinion, cannot be compensated by any other natural advantage.

As to the people or inhabitants, their souls are engrossed by lucre, and [they] are very expert in affairs of merchandise; but as to politeness, it is a thing banished from their republic as a contagious distemper. This is an article which cannot be well excused, as it seldom costs much. If they are not hospitable, allowances may be made for it, as it is partly owing to the genius or disposition of a people.

I think I have touched upon the most remarkable places in Briſtol. A perſon may ſuſpect my being prejudiced towards them, but really I only ſpeak as I found it, and poſſibly another may find it quite contrary. I have heard of the moſt polite place being accounted diſagreeable, and it is certain that by an ill concurring of circumſtances theſe events may be produced.

I ſhall not ſay how my time paſſed here, which was much longer than I expected, but at length the joyful news arrived that the ſhip was ready to ſail. The captain deſired us to go down to Pile ; we took a boat and our farewell of this enchanting place ; we paſſed through many mountains, which ſeemed to impend over us ; we arrived at Pile at ſix o'clock (a poor mean place), and next morning at ſix ſaw the veſſel at her moorings. When the tide ſerved, they hoiſted the flag, at which ſignal we took boat and went on board. We had not remained long here when another boat boarded us, in which we found a couple of gentlemen and a lady, who were alſo paſſengers. Was I in the boat when ſhe came up the veſſel's ſide, I doubt not but I ſhould have been ſomething concerned, as the wind, which blew ſomewhat hard, diſconcerted her petticoats. However, ſhe ſurmounted this difficulty, and ſeemed pleaſed that nothing worſe had happened.

I was impatient to know who this fair paffenger was, and, as I thought it would render my voyage the more agreeable, I refolved to introduce myfelf to her as fpeedily as poffible, and for that purpofe advanced to the feat where fhe placed herfelf. I accofted her according to the common method, and was furprifed to find myfelf anfwered in the moft polite terms with fuch a volubility of tongue and a franknefs fo natural that I conjectured it muft have required uncommon pains to arrive at this perfection. Tho' I endeavoured to correct my brogue, yet fome irregular pronunciations flipped from me, which the good-natured creature corrected with an engaging affability which made fuch an impreffion on my mind that I am confident I fhall never miftake in the fame points again. I was happy enough to find fomething to fpeak of for a few minutes that engaged her attention, but then my bad fate drove one of the gentlemen (who came with her) to our fide, at which I withdrew, as I found fhe had an inclination to talk on more refined topics than fhe found me mafter of; and [I] took my ftand where I could conveniently hear.

He, fmiling upon her, afked how fhe bore the thoughts of returning to Ireland. At this a gloom overfpread her countenance, and with downcaſt eyes [ſhe] ſaid it would be time enough to experience afflićtion when it came, and not to increaſe it ſooner, and, added ſhe, with a ſigh,— "Oh, London, thou ſweeteſt of places ! every moment I am ſtill carried further from thee. When ſhall I ſee a play, an opera, a maſquerade, a Vauxhall, a Ranelagh, a St. James's drawing-room ? Sad, ſad reflećtion ! ill-natured brute to call to remembrance ſuch delights, ſuch pleaſures, afforded in a place where I cannot be ! My mornings now, how will they be ſpent ? perhaps poring over ſome ſtupid book, without a park or public breakfaſt, to be obliged to dreſs in the uncouth manner of the inhabitants, when what little ſtock of new ones I have now are exhauſted. Mortifying thought ! No Garrick to melt the ſoul in tragic ſtrain—no ſerenade to gently break my ſlumbers, except the ruder voice of a neighbouring peaſant's cock ! " In uttering theſe laſt words her head fell into a languiſhing poſture, and the court-lady reigned in every ačtion.

> " Prаčtiſ'd to liſp and hang the head aſide,
> Faints into airs and languiſhes with pride."
>
> POPE.

I did not wait to hear the gentleman's defence after the rude ſhock he had given this unfortu-

nate lady, but went down to my cabin under
great anxiety left he fhould find a punifhment
fuitable to his crime. I foon came on deck again,
by which time all our fails were bent, and we
ftood out with a fair wind. We had a fine profpect all the day of England on the left hand and
Wales on the right. We foon ouftripped two
other veffels that failed the fame tide with us. In
the evening by ill luck our main topfail-yard
broke, by which means our going was fomething
retarded. Towards night, the fea running pretty
high, I was obliged to betake [myfelf] to my
cabin becaufe of the prodigious ficknefs. But, oh
Gods! judge of my defpair when I faw the lady
lying in the ftate-room as if dead. This redouble-
ment of my griefs caufed emotions in my whole
frame, and had near exhaufted all my ftrength
before I got any relief, and what added to my
trouble was that I could afford her no other [at-
tention] than by faintly calling fometimes to her.
In the morning I grew pretty hearty, and before
noon was entirely well.

This day and the next night elapfed before the
lady got an abatement of her malady, when by
adminiftering fome broth and green tea fhe recovered her fpirits, but we could not perfuade her
to arife. The gentleman conftantly kept her

company, and by liftening to her converfation I gained a better tafte for the polite world, excepting one point in pronunciation, to wit, that of calling A E and faying EE for E ; but this was a thing I could not readily reconcile myfelf to, for I remember when I firft went to fchool my miftrefs made me begin with my great A. Whether it was that the letter was bigger in dimenfions than its brother vowel E that followed it, I cannot tell, but I am very certain fhe never made me fay great E. I was fo very defective, or [failed] by too blunt a clipping, that my fair tutorefs faid fhe was afraid I would never make any hand on't. She affured me fhe was not above eight or ten months arriving at that perfection which I am fure would coft me my whole life without making half her progrefs.

I think I have heard fay an ape is the moft ridiculous of beafts, as it hath nothing genuine, but borrows its tricks from others. Whether it would not be commendable to conform to what we are firft initiated in, is a point very few will difpute.

Next morning one of the failors came down with the joyful tidings that he defcried land. This elated my fpirits, as I was anxious to be afhore ; but a thick fog arifing denied us the

pleafing profpect of Ireland. About eleven the
wind veered about, and prevented us making the
harbour of Cork. The fog continuing, we had
juft run afhore, had not one of the men perceived
the land, and immediately we caft anchor. At
mid-day the fun unmantled himfelf, and exhaled
moft part of the offenfive fog, when, to our
great joy, we found ourfelves oppofite the harbour of Youghal. We efpied a fifhing-boat at a
diftance, for which we hung out the pavilion.
She immediately obeyed the fignal. The captain
faid he could not make the intended port that
night, whereupon the paffengers agreed to go
afhore in the boat. With fome difficulty we
defcended into her, and in lefs than a half an
hour got to the quay, where we fafely landed :—

"Optatâ potiuntur arenâ."—VIRG.

We made here a hearty breakfaft, after which
my father and I took horfes, and arrived in Cork
about nine at night. I fhall now put a period to
my tedious defcription, and omit my return to
Dublin, which I may hereafter fpeak of, thereby
to make out the circle.

FINIS.

NOTES.

Page 12. *Liverpool Harbour.*

FOR an infight into the early ftate of Liverpool there are three excellent authorities, namely, *A Journey through England in* 1714, by John Macky, of which Mr. Halliwell has given as much as relates to Liverpool in his *Palatine Anthology*, 1850, pp. 27-28; *A Tour through the Whole Ifland of Great Britain*, by Daniel Defoe, 6th edit. 1761, iii. p. 240, *et feq.*; and Brooke's *Defcriptive account of Liverpool during the laft Quarter of the* 18*th Century*, 1775-1800. *Liverpool*, 1853. Roy. 8vo.

The following from Defoe's narrative, which firft appeared in 1724, is fomewhat to the purpofe, as probably matters were not greatly improved in 1752:—" You land on the flat fhore on the other fide [of the Merfey], and muft be content to ride thro' the Water for fome Length, not on Horfeback, but on the fhoulders of fome *Lancafhire* Clown, who comes knee deep to the Boat's fide to trufs you up, and then runs away more nimble than one defires to ride, unlefs his Trot were eafier."

P. 14. *Liverpool Docks.* "They have made a fine dock here [at Liverpool] for the fecurity of their fhipping, where fourfcore fail of fhips may lie in the greateft ftorms, as fecure as a man in his bed. But this is all forced, nothing of nature; and when they have brought frefh water into the town, which

is defigned, by pipes from fome fprings in Sir Cleve More's eftate, about four miles off, and for which they have got an Act of Parliament, may become one of the fineft towns in England."
—Macky's *Journey through England in* 1714.

P. 19. *An Eightpenny Ordinary.* In 1720, according to *A Vade Mecum for Malt Worms,* part ii. p. 30, there was fuch an ordinary at the Bell Inn, in Carter Lane; but the landlord, finding that it did not pay, raifed his charge to ten-pence, which, unlefs his bill of fare was fuperior to that of fuch inftitutions in our day, ftrikes one (confidering the dif-ference in prices and the value of money) as rather high. From the title of one of Rowlands's tracts, printed in 1600 (*Humors Ordinarie, where a man may be verie merrie, and exceeding well vfed for his Sixe-Pence*) it is perhaps allowable to infer, that in the clofing years of Queen Elizabeth's reign, fixpence was the ufual demand at the metropolitan *tables d'hote.*

P. 22. *Economy of Human Life.* This is, of courfe, Dodf-ley's poem fo called. It was at the time when the prefent narrative was compofed in the enjoyment of a certain fhare of popularity, being a comparatively new book, and, befides, erroneoufly afcribed to Lord Chefterfield at the time of pub-lication. The firft edition appeared in 1750.

P. 30. *I led my Statira back.* Statira, it may perhaps be neceffary to remind the reader, is the heroine of Calprenede's once exceffively popular, but now altogether forgotten, Pla-tonic romance of *Caffandra,* which remained in favour from the middle of the feventeenth till the end of the laft century, or even the commencement of the prefent. But the romantic literature of the feventeenth century was rather eclipfed (in a popular fenfe) by the novels (chiefly tranflations) which made their appearance in Swift's and Pope's day, and were by no means fo unexceptionable as their predeceffors, even if fome-what livelier. Thefe again were fuperfeded by the productions of the Duke de la Rochefoucauld, Madame de la Fayette, and

that clafs of writers, whom we ought not perhaps to be furprifed to find a man like Gray devouring with delight, when
we bear in mind that our grandfathers were fimilarly infatuated
with the productions of the Minerva Prefs, and that we ourfelves are feeding on an article ftill lefs healthy.

P. 34. *Perkin a Legh.* The Perkin a Legh here mentioned was Sir Piers Legh, fecond fon of Robert Legh, of
Adlington. He efpoufed, as the monumental record informs
us, the caufe of Richard II., and perifhed on the fcaffold at
Chefter, 23 Rich. II. His fon, alfo referred to here, was Sir
Peter Legh of Lyme, 'knight banneret, and grantee of the
borough and manor. He was wounded at Agincourt, died at
Paris, and was carried over to England for fepulture at Macclesfield. See Ormerod's *Hiftory of Chefhire,* iii. 336-8, 367.

Sir Peter Legh of Lyme, reftorer of the old ftone in the
reign of James I. was the fon of Peter Legh, Efq., who died
vitâ patris, and grandfon of Sir Peter Legh of Lyme and
Haydock, who was knighted by Henry VIII. at Leith. Sir
Peter himfelf died in 1636.

It may be mentioned that Perkin (*forfan* Peterkin) a Legh
was the perfon to whom has been fometimes improperly given
the credit really due to his father-in-law, Sir Thomas Dan-
yers, of having, on the field of Creçy, taken prifoner the
Chamberlain of France.

P. 35. *Rivers' Chapel.* See Ormerod's *Hiftory of Chefhire,*
iii. 336, 368. The families of Legh of Lyme and Savage
(Earls Rivers) intermarried.

P. 44. *Scraping.* Valerius followed a fafhion which Beaumont feems to ridicule in *The Faithfull Friends,* where
Flavia fays of Sir Pergamus—" At firft encounter he fcraped
me a leg that fet my teeth on edge." At the time when this
tour was written, many Englifh cuftoms remained unaltered,
or very flightly modified, from the form under which they
had exifted in Beaumont and Fletcher's own day.

P. 49. *The little fun-flies feemed delighted, and, gilded*

fport, &c. I at firft fufpected a flip of the pen here, and that
we ought to read *glided in fport;* but I conclude that the
writer intended to convey that the funlight gilded the flies.
Compare Tennyfon—

> " Many a night I faw the Pleiads, rifing through the mellow fhade,
> Glitter like a fwarm of fire-flies tangled in a filver braid."
>
> *Lockfley Hall.*

P. 57. *Leek.* At the time our traveller vifited this place, it
was furrounded by moors.

P. 57. *Afhborne.* This place is ten miles from Derby (our
tourift makes it twelve), and is on the borders of Staffordfhire.

P. 63. *King Richard III., who was there interred.* Lewis
(*Topographical Dictionary,* art. LEICESTER) obferves—" In the
fouth-weftern part [of the town] was a convent of Francifcan
or Grey Friars, founded in 1265 by Simon de Montfort, in
the church of which was interred the body of Richard III.
after his death at the battle of Bofworth Field."

Richard is faid to have flept on the night before the battle
at or near Leicefter, on a bed which is ftill preferved at Beaumanor Park, near Loughborough. This bed, which bears
marks of having received additions about the time of Elizabeth
or James I., was, in all probability, in Richard's time (affuming
it to be genuine), a fort of truckle-bed, which was folded up
when not in ufe. The curious relic at Beaumanor was purchafed by its prefent owner, after having been in the Drake
and Babington families upwards of two centuries. It continued
to form part of the furniture of the Blue Boar at Leicefter as
late as 1610; and it is well known that the landlady of that
houfe, having difcovered a large quantity of gold coin infide the
mattrefs, was murdered, and that the affaffins were hanged at
Leicefter for the crime.

It is hardly neceffary to add that the authenticity of the
legend has been gravely queftioned, and certainly the evi-
dence in its favour is purely traditional. The carving at the

head, which probably formed part of the original bed, is a reprefentation of the Holy Trinity ; it is, no doubt (whatever its hiftory may have been), fifteenth-century work, and a very interefting fpecimen of the ornamental ftyle of that period. See further, as to Richard III. and the field of Bofworth, Kelly's *Leicefter in the Olden Time*, 1865, p. 92, *note.*

P. 64. *By a late Act of Parliament.* The Act here referred to was, however, merely a declaratory one, with additional reftrictions, as on the 16th Auguft, 1661, we find a procla-mation iffued by Charles II. " to reftrain the exceffive car-riages in wagons and four-wheeled carts to the deftruction of highways." There was a further proclamation concerning highways in 1671. The tax on *loaded* vehicles was not re-pealed, it appears, in 1794 (Gunning's *Reminifcences of Cam-bridge*, i. 338).

P. 68. *Newport-Pagnell.* " Newport-Pagnell is a large, well-built, populous town, feated on the river Ouze, over which it has two large ftone bridges. It carries on a great trade in bone-lace, and the fame manufacture employs alfo the neighbouring villages."—*Tour through the Whole Ifland of Great Britain*, 1761, ii. 231. The travellers muft have made a long circuit to take Newport-Pagnell in their way. Their route, as we fee, lay through the midland counties, Nottinghamfhire, Leicefterfhire, Northamptonfhire, Bedford-fhire, Hertfordfhire, and fo to London; and therefore how they got round to Buckinghamfhire it is hard to divine—un-lefs, indeed, in their homeward journey, which they made through Berkfhire, Buckinghamfhire, &c. There is fome miftake, which cannot now be cleared up, perhaps, even if it were worth the procefs.

P. 71. *Infignificant*, i. e., deftitute of meaning.

P. 72. *What the Earl of Orrery hath faid of him in a late treatife.* The book here referred to was called *Remarks on the Life and Writings of Dr. Jonathan Swift*, Lond. 1751, 8vo. the author being John Boyle, Earl of Cork and Orrery. His lordſhip addreſſed theſe remarks in a ſeries of letters to his ſon. It is ſaid that 12,000 copies were ſold; there were certainly two or three editions. Warburton characterizes the Letters as "deteſtable."

P. 75. *Oborn.* Either the tranſcriber of the MS. made a ſlip of the pen here (only one among many), or the author himſelf muſt have miſ-heard the name of the place through which he and his friends were paſſing. Of courſe *Woburn* is the village intended; it is ſituated within a ſhort diſtance of Hockliffe or Hockley-in-the-Hole. Both are in the Hundred of Manſhead, co. Bedford, on the old high road to Yorkſhire. Woburn itſelf ſeems to be a corruption of *Womborn.* Womburn, co. Stafford, preſerves the genuine form of the name. The *Tour through the Whole Iſland of Great Britain,* 1761, iii. 51, ſays—"Woburn, noted for having plenty of fuller's earth near it, and likewiſe another kind of earth, which petrifies wood into ſtone. This town, having been almoſt demoliſhed by a terrible fire, which happened a few years ago, is now rebuilt, and makes no mean appearance. It belongs almoſt all of it to his grace the Duke of Bedford, who finiſhed in Feb., 1737, a fine and commodious market-place here. This place is famous for jockey-caps."

P. 75. *Hockley-in-the-Hole.* The latter is deſcribed in a contemporary publication (*England's Gazetteer,* 1751,) as "in a miry road to Coventry, 5 m. beyond Dunſtable." This road was notorious in the time of Queen Elizabeth for its badneſs.

> "A Ballad entituled A newe Well a daye,
> As playne, maiſter papiſt, as Dunſtable waye,"

was printed about 1570, and is included among *Ancient Ballads and Broadſides,* 1867. It may be ſuſpected, however, that the true reading of this proverbial phraſe was loſt at an early date; for John Heywood, in his work on Proverbs, printed by Berthelet in 1546, gives us what was evidently the original ſentence:—"as plain as Dunſtable *by*-way."

P. 75. *'Em.* This is a fort of elliplis for *the footpads.* Our author is juftified by our elder writers here :—

> " *Ifabella.* Why did you not anfwer 'em ?
> *Lady Hartwell.* They are fo impudent they will receive *none.*"
>> Fletcher's *Wit without Money* (1614.)

P. 78. *Monument erected to the memory of the good Duke Humphrey,* The writer's account may be compared with that given by Stow, in his *Survey,* ed. Strype, 1720, book iii. p. 165, where the error refpecting the interment of the Duke of Gloucefter at St. Paul's, London, is pointed out.

P. 78. *As Duke Humphrey,* &c. An account of the myfterious death of the Duke of Gloucefter may be found in the writers of the time.

P. 81. *Finchley Common, fo celebrated for the frequent robberies,* &c. Our open fpaces in the fuburbs of London, and even in the metropolis itfelf, have not yet quite loft the unenviable diftinction, which they enjoyed to the fulleft extent, when our Tourift wrote. Even in the earlier part of the prefent century, Hounflow, Bagfhot, and Putney Heaths, and all the other commons about London, were abfolutely unfafe for fingle travellers, and people traverfed them in parties. See Andrews' *Eighteenth Century,* 1856, chap. 14, where fome interefting details on this fubject may be found ; alfo, *A Hundred Years Ago,* 1857, by James Hutton, p. 243, *et feqq.* Thefe two works traverfe the fame ground, and are precifely fimilar in character and object, but muft be fuppofed to have been written independently of each other.

P. 81. *High Gate. Here it is that they are fworn to feveral comical oaths.* The writer alludes, of courfe, to the well known but now obfolete ufage of making people freemen of Highgate. There is an old rhyme :—

> " It's a cuftom at Highgate, that all who go through,
> Muft be fworn on the horns, fir, and fo fir, muft you ;
> Bring the horns, fhut the door ; now, fir, off with your hat ;
> And when you again come, pray don't forget that."

This is, however, merely a counterpart of an old continental custom, according to Dr. Bell (*Shakespeare's Puck*, i. 15). "Highgate derives its name from a gate set up there above 400 years ago, to receive toll for the Bishop of London, when the old miry road from Gray's-Inn-Lane to Barnet was turned through the Bishop's park."—*England's Gazetteer*, 1751, in voce.

P. 81. *Tory.* Tory was the old term in Ireland for a robber or thief, and its political meaning was merely a new application of the word as a party nickname.

> " I went to the wood,
> And killed a tory ;
> I went to the wood,
> And killed another ;
> Was it himself, or was it his brother ? "
>
> *The Laird of Logan.*

P. 83. *Reminded me of Strap.* The parallel (or *supposed* parallel) incident is to be found at ch. 13, of *Roderic Random*, where Roderic and Strap arrive in London, are insulted in the streets, &c. The passage is too long and, besides, too well known to bear citation here.

P. 85. *The Royal Exchange.* A view of the old Exchange will be found in Strype's edit. of Stow's *Survey*, 1720, book ii. p. 135. At p. 137, Strype gives a slightly varying account of the devices on the pedestal :—" On the top of this inscription [*Carolo Cæsari*, &c.] a crown, adorned with palm branches, scepter, sword, and trumpets of Fame. On the west side of the pedestal, a boy winged, laying his right hand upon the crown set over the arms of *England*, and holding in its left a branch with two roses, viz., of *York* and *Lancaster*. On the north side, the like boy with wings holding the crown, resting upon the *Irish* Harp. On the east side, the winged boy holding the arms of *Scotland*, crowned, having a thistle, with the stalk in his right hand.

P. 86. *The Court of Hustings.* Of this ancient institution

fee a long defcription in Strype's edition of Stow's *Survey of London*, 1720, lib. v. p. 369. It is faid, doubtlefs correctly, to derive its name from Anglo-Saxon *Hus* and *thing*, i. e., the houfe of pleas or caufes. Stow fpeaks of this court as "the ancienteft and the higheft Court of Juftice of the famous City of *London*."

P. 88. *Acroteria.* "Small pedeftals placed on the middle, and two ends of pediments to fupport ftatues."—*Gwilt.*

P. 94-5. *Vauxhall Gardens.* The manor and manorhoufe of Vauxhall, previoufly known as Copped, or Copt Hall, to which thefe grounds were originally attached, belonged to Jane Vaux, widow of John Vaux, citizen and vintner of London (in no way related, I believe, to the Fawkes's of Yorkfhire), in the reign of James I. But in a deed of Edward II.'s time (1319) the place is called *Faukef-hall*, which makes, perhaps, a flight difficulty in deciding whether the manor really owed its denomination either to the Fawkes or Vaux families. When our Tourift and his friend paid a vifit to them in 1752, they had been opened as a public place of recreation about twenty years, although it appears that they had, as early as 1681, ceafed to be a private demefne, and were then known as the *Spring Gardens*, under which title the *Spectator* refers to them in 1711. Ranelagh does not feem to have long furvived the rife of Vauxhall.

The moft copious hiftorical account of Vauxhall is to be found in Mr. Tanfwell's interefting *Hiftory of Lambeth*, 1858, p. 176-7. In Johnfon's *Lottery Song-Book* are collected the fongs which ufed to be principally in favour at this famous place of entertainment.

P. 99. *Spitalfields.* The MS. reads *Spittle Fields*, which perfectly coincides with the old way of fpeaking of the place. Thefe fields formerly belonged to the Hofpital, (in old Englifh, *Spyttel*) and Priory of St. Bartholomew in Smithfield. There is an early poem by Robert Copland, the literary printer, entitled, *The Hye Way to the Spyttel Hous* (i.e., St. Bartholomew's). It was publifhed in 1532, and may be found inferted in *Remains of the Early Popular Poetry of England*, iv.

" In the afternoone we walked to the Old Artillery Ground, near to the Spitalfields, where I never was before, but now, by Captain Deane's invitation, did go to fee his new gun tryed ; this being the place where the officers of the ordnance do try all their great guns."—Pepys' *Diary*, April 20, 1669.

P. 100. *Ranelagh*. The author of *A Tour through the whole Ifland of Great Britain*, firft publifhed in 1724, and re-edited with additions in 1761, (a few years after the date of the *Journey*), fays of the late feat of the Earl of Ranelagh, then recently converted into a pleafure garden :—" The manfion is now turned into a breakfafting houfe, and dedicated to that luxury which overfpreads the nation. A rotonda, as I may call it, is erected in the gardens, to propagate found inftead of fenfe, and to feaft the eyes of belles and beaux, who croud thither to become fpectacles to one another, for the benefit of the proprietors of the undertaking. . . . *Marybone Gardens*, *Sadler's Wells*, and a variety of fuch fort of houfes of entertainment about *Iflington*, hardly to be numbered, and all boafting of their bands of *Mufic*, befides what I have taken notice of in other places, are emanations, as I may call them, from the two grand feminaries of luxury, *Ranelagh* and *Vaux Hall Gardens*."

Mrs. Delany, in a letter to Mrs. Dewes, April 26, 1744, fays, " Yefterday, my brother gallantly attended Mrs. Donnellan, Mifs Dafhwood, and myfelf to breakfaft at Ranelagh ; the day was clear but cold ; there was a great deal of company."—*Autobiography and Correfpondence of Mrs. Delany*, 1ft feries, ii. 299. See alfo Mr. Cunningham's edition of Walpole's *Letters*, i. 158, and the fame gentleman's *Handbook of London*, 1849.

In Gunning's *Reminifcences of Cambridge*, i. 207-8, there is a curious account of a notorious pickpocket, named Barrington, who ufed to infeft Ranelagh, and to whom the ladies always, rightly or wrongly, fet down their frequent and ferious loffes of valuable trinkets.

P. 101. *Chelfea Bun Houfe.* See Cunningham's *Handbook of London, Paft and Prefent,* 1849. This houfe, which ftood at the bottom of Jews' Row, was taken down in 1839.

P. 104. *As I met 'em fomewhere tranflated by an eminent hand.* The " eminent hand" was evidently the common fource to which both Chamberlain in his *Angliæ Notitia,* and Strype, in his edition of Stow's Survey, 1720, went for this verfion of the Latin. Stow gives only one paragraph, omitted by Chamberlain, and apparently refers us to the *Notitia* for the reft.

P. 108. *London Bridge.* The houfes which the writer defcribes as having feen on the bridge, were removed four or five years afterwards. In Brayley's *Londiniana,* ii. 256, is an account of the appearance of London Bridge in 1755. In a view of London in 1657, which forms the frontifpiece to the fame volume, the river and bridge occur, and a good idea may be gained of the afpeft of the old ftruƈture, which did not change its charaƈter or form very materially till the demolition of the buildings at the date above-mentioned.

P. 110. *A particular furvey of the Lions,* &c. Of this intended publication there is no *exaƈt* trace ; it was probably never printed, and has perifhed, or at leaft difappeared from view, but at any time may turn up as unexpeƈtedly as the MS., which records its exiftence. It is to be feared, that its literary importance would not be very confiderable ; but it might affift in identifying *Valerius,* and poffibly through him, the author of the *Journey.* I ought to add, that in 1753, appeared a traƈt entitled, *A Hiftorical defcription of the Tower of London and its Curiofities,* 8vo. price 6*d.* Can this have been the *Treatife* for which Valerius made notes the year before ?

I have met with no fewer than three editions of this fmall volume ; the firft defcribed in the Britifh Mufeum Catalogue

as of (1750), but without the title-page; a fecond edition in
1755, and a third in 1774. There is unluckily no clue to the
authorfhip, unlefs we regard as one the fpeciality which the
writer makes of the Tower Menagerie, which formed, as we
know from the *Journey*, the leading attraction in the eyes of
Valerius. The Regalia are alfo defcribed at confiderable
length, as they are in the fmall volume now printed.

From an advertifement on the laft page of the edition of
1774, it appears that the defcription was tranflated into French,
prior to that year (*depuis peu de temps*), and publifhed at 1*s.*

At the fale of Mr. George Smith's books, in 1867, a copy of
this fixpenny tract (edition not fpecified) produced 3*l.* 11*s.*
See *Notes and Queries* for January 2, 1869. It appears to
have wanted the title.

P. 111. *A lift of his Majefty's regalia.* A more particular
account of the regalia is to be found in *An Hiftorical Defcription of the Tower,* &c., 1753, ed. 1755, p. 63.

P. 113. *Invincible Armada—different kinds of fetters,* &c.
Deloney, a popular ballad-writer of the period, when the
Armada muft have been the topic of all topics, undertook
to defcribe in one of the doggrel compofitions which are the
fpeciality of the craft " the ftraunge and cruell whippes which
the Spanyards had prepared to Whippe and torment Englifh
men and women, which were found and taken at the ouer-
throw of certaine of the Spanifhe Shippes in July laft paft,
1588." Thefe whips do not appear to have found their way
to the Tower.

P. 113. *Ampulla.* This is ftrictly nothing more than a
bottle with a narrow neck, and was in ufe among the Romans
as an ordinary veffel for holding liquids. The few perfons
whofe eyes the prefent volume is likely to meet fcarcely require to be told that in Rome and Greece, and afterwards in
modern Europe, drinking-cups and flagons were commonly
executed in the forms of animals (dogs, bears, birds, etc.) See
Fairholt's *Mifcellanea Graphica,* 1857, plates vi. xi. xiv.

P. 113. *Curtana.* The Curtana, or Curteyn, was the name of the fword of Edward the Confeffor, and is the firft fword carried before the kings of England at their coronation ; and it is faid the point of it is broken as an emblem of mercy. —Tomline's *Law Diſt., voce* CURTEYN.

P. 115. *Lord Kinſale.* The family ſtill poſſeſſes this right, but it is virtually nominal, and, it is believed, has never been exerciſed. The barony of Kinſale, Ireland, is ſaid to have been the firſt Iriſh peerage conferred on an Engliſhman, and Lord Kinſale is the premier baron of Ireland. As a barony by tenure, the title dates back to the Norman Conqueſt.

P. 115. *John of Gaunt, the French general.* So the MS. reads. The coat of armour, &c., to which our touriſt here refers, belonged apparently to John de Courcy, firſt Earl of Ulſter, of that family, who in the reign of King John was raiſed to this dignity for his ſervices in the reduction of Ulſter. The writer appears to have fallen into utter confuſion when he ſpeaks of John of Gaunt, &c., who lived nearly two centuries later, and was aſſuredly never " the French general" on any occaſion whatever. The exploit which gained for the Lords Kinſale the privilege referred to was of a totally different character from that repreſented in the text. See Sharpe's Peerage, art. KINSALE.

P. 118. *Cuper's Gardens.* Or more correctly Cuper's Garden. This was ſituated at Lambeth, near what is now known as the Waterloo Bridge Road, on the river-ſide, and formerly belonged to the Howards, Dukes of Norfolk and Earls of Arundel. Boydell Cuper, who had been gardener to Thomas Howard, Earl of Arundel, collector of the marbles which are ſtill known as the Arundelian, and are by his be-queſt preſerved at Oxford, obtained on the demolition of Arundel Houſe, in the Strand, ſome of the imperfect ſtatuary, and removed it to this place, which he converted into grounds for public recreation. In 1717 his ſon, John Cuper, ſold the ancient fragments, but the garden continued for many years

longer to be a refort for pleafure-feekers. The fite is now
occupied by narrow ftreets, but was at one time covered by
Beaufoy's great wine manufaĉtory. See Brayley and Britton's
Hift. of Surrey, iii. 334. Kennington, Lambeth, Camberwell,
and other outlying localities bordering on the metropolis, have
always been celebrated for their tea-gardens, which have not
invariably borne the beft charaĉter. The fulleft particulars of
Cuper's Garden, tracing back its hiftory to a very remote
period, may be found in Mr. Tanfwell's *Hiftory of Lambeth*,
1858, p. 180. Cuper's Gardens were very much the fame
as Cremorne Gardens in our time ; the amufements confifted
of dancing, finging, mufic, fireworks, &c., and at the outfet,
I believe, a leading attraĉtion was a Mr. Jones, who performed
with aftonifhing fkill (as it was thought) on the Welfh harp.

P. 119. *Weftminfter Bridge.* This was the ugly ftone
ftruĉture lately demolifhed to make room for the fplendid
bridge now completed. The *old* bridge (as we fhould call it)
had itfelf fuperfeded a timber one, of which the ereĉtion com-
menced, after a good deal of confultation, in 1737. The
works were under the fuperintendence of a commiffion, the
members of which, for fome very exquifite reafon doubtlefs,
deliberately gave wood the preference to ftone. See a humo-
rous fatire on the wooden bridge at Weftminfter and its
authors in Dodfley's Colleĉtion of Poems, edit. 1782, iii. 7.

P. 119. *Awful.* In the fenfe of awe-infpiring.

P. 121. *One Bell in the Strand.* I do not know whether
this was a hoftelry of any confequence ; but, at all events, I
do not find it enumerated among the places of note in this
way in a *Vade Mecum for Malt Worms* (1720).

P. 122. *The new church.* St. Martin's-in-the-Fields. See
Stow's *Survey of London*, ed. 1720, book vi. pp. 69, 73.
This new church had been confecrated in 1726.

P. 126. *Our coach went on as faft as the pavements would
admit.* An extraordinary piĉture of the ftate of the highways
at this period is fupplied in a work which was printed in

1768, *A Six Weeks' Tour through the Southern Counties of England and Wales*, 8vo. This narrative embraces a description of some of the suburban roads out of London ; and those within the area of the metropolis were, even within the memory of those still living, not a whit superior. Those who were acquainted with Manchester before the introduction of recent improvements, or with Rouen or Antwerp, or many other continental towns, as they still remain, can form a tolerably fair idea of the condition of the London thoroughfares prior to the present century, and indeed some way into the latter. Swift, in his *Journal*, gives a pitiful account of his travelling experiences in London and the outskirts.

Gunning, describing the state of the streets in Cambridge in 1794, says—"The wretched state of the streets had long been a disgrace to the university and town of Cambridge. The gutters were in the middle of the streets, in several of which it was impossible for two carriages to pass each other " (*Reminiscences*, 1854, i. 319). Yet Charles II., in the first year of his reign, issued a proclamation for the improvement of the streets in London and Westminster.

The travelling-carriages of this date, besides a place behind for the footman, were provided with accommodation of some kind for two servants, whose special business it was to help, when required, in extricating the vehicle or the horses, or both, from ruts, &c. An equipage of this description, built in 1741 in Long Acre, recently came under my notice ; it was a wedding-coach, and though undoubtedly a curious relic, struck the eye as singularly unwieldy. Labour was then comparatively cheap ; this carriage cost 95*l.*, equal, perhaps, to about 160*l.* of our money ; and such another could not be constructed at the present time under 300*l.*

P. 135. *Marlborough Downs.* "I am now come into the road to Marlborough. On the downs, about two or three miles from the town, are abundance of stones lying scattered about the plain, some whereof are very large. . . . They are called by the country-people the *Grey Wethers,* and it muſt be confeſſed that they look not unlike ſheep ſtraggling upon the downs on a tranſient and diſtant view as travellers paſs. Theſe *Grey Wethers,* on a more curious inſpečtion, are found to be a ſort of white marble, and lie upcn the ſurface of the ground in infinite numbers, and of all dimenſions."—*A Tour through Great Britain,* &c., edit. 1761, ii. 49-50.

P. 139. *Bath.* A good deſcription of this town, as it appeared in the firſt half of the laſt century, may be found in *A Tour through Great Britain,* &c., edit. 1761, ii. 285, *et ſeq.* There is alſo a tolerably copious account of it in a contemporary and very excellent little work called *England's Gazetteer,* 1751, 3 vols. 12mo.

P. 155. *Calling A E, and ſaying EE for E.* The pronunciation of A for E, as *Phædrus* for *Phædrus,* is ſtill an Iriſh idioſyncraſy; but as regards the latter part of the propoſition, it is curious enough that Lye, who was afterwards Archdeacon of Totneſs, recommends, in his very rare *Spelling-Book,* printed about 1690, the ſounding of E as if it were reduplicated, in words like *England,* &c. I am not aware that the opinion is one which has received ſupport among philologiſts, but our Iriſh fellow-countrymen certainly reduce the principle to praĉtice, without being conſcious, perhaps, that it has received ſanĉtion in print.[1]

---

[1] A New Spelling Book, or Reading and Spelling Engliſh made eaſie, wherein all the Words of Our Engliſh Bible are ſet down in Alphabetical Order, and divided into diſtinĉt Syllables, together with the Grounds of the Engliſh Tongue, laid in Piĉtures, Words, and Verſe, wherein are Couched many Moral Precepts. By the Help whereof (with God's Bleſſing) Little Children and others of Ordinary Capacities, may, in few months be enabled exaĉtly to read and ſpell the whole Bible. The Fourth Edition. By Thomas Lye, Philanglus. London, Printed for Thomas Parkhurſt, at the Bible and Three Crowns in Cheapſide, near Mercers Chapel, 16[90]. Small 8vo., with woodcuts.

INDEX.

The MS. which has been employed, already contained an Index; but the latter was of so unsatisfactory a character, that it was thought better to prepare a fresh one.

www.ingramcontent.com/pod-product-compliance
Lightning Source LLC
Chambersburg PA
CBHW030610040726

47497CB00008B/2926